VISITS

VISITS

DAVE MCINTOSH

On the road to things past

Stoddart

First published in 1990 by
Stoddart Publishing Co. Limited
34 Lesmill Road
Toronto, Canada
M3B 2T6

CANADIAN CATALOGUING IN PUBLICATION DATA

McIntosh, Dave.
    Visits: on the road to things past

ISBN 0-7737-2428-1

1. McIntosh, Dave.   2. Canada — History — 1914-1945.
3. Canada — History — 1945-   .   4. Authors,
Canadian (English) — Biography.*   5. Canadian Press
Association — Biography.   6. Canadian wit and humor
(English).*   1. Title.

FC601.M25A3 1990   971.06'092   C90-094524-9
F1034.3.M25A3 1990

DESIGN: Brant Cowie/ArtPlus Limited

Printed and bound in Canada

To those well met on the road,
especially Jean

Contents

VISITS

Recruiting Drive

In the summer of 1940, when I was almost nineteen, I got a job caddying at Jasper Park Lodge. I kidded myself that I was hired on my qualifications, though I knew perfectly well that my mother had a friend pretty high up at Canadian National Railways, which owned and ran the lodge. I had put in a lot of time caddying, but more time playing—in the 1930s, customers were scarce. My course was Dufferin Heights Country Club, a nine-holer four miles from my home in Stanstead, Quebec. There were few calls for our services during the week and the number of caddies shrank to two or three, the others preferring to go swimming instead of horsing around the caddy shack (actually, the tool shed) in the faint hopes of making 35 cents for nine holes, 60 cents for 18. Only during a big weekend tournament could you count on raking in 60 cents, and some bigshot might add a 15-cent tip if you washed the ball often and exclaimed "Good shot, sir" at every one of his 150-yard drives.

Summer jobs were hard to come by and you couldn't hope for much more than one that provided room and board. In the summer of 1939 I worked on a one-horse farm that included half-a-dozen lakeside cabins near Georgeville, not far from home. Part of my job was raking the beach every morning to make sure there were no large or sharp stones for the tender feet of the cabin-renters to step on. I was paid 10 dollars a month besides room and board, the room being a tool shed that I shared with another hired hand.

I spent a lot of my youth in tool sheds. I nearly drowned in one. I was running away from a big and ferocious boy on the way home from school and sought shelter in a tool shed behind the green house next to the Anglican church. The shed harbored the cesspool (the sewer was yet to come to Stanstead), and the top had been taken off so that it could be drained and relined (I found out afterwards). I banged the door shut behind me and leaped for a corner hiding place. I leaped directly into the cesspool, which fortunately was full to within two feet or so of the top, allowing me to scramble out, though with considerable difficulty and covered in stinking slime. I waited until my pursuer had given up his search and I went down to the swimming hole in the Tomifobia River behind the school and lay, fully clothed, in the running water until most of the filth let go. I dried off in the sun on the way home. "What's that I smell?" my mother asked. "David, where have you been?" "I fell down at Carroll's," I said. Carroll LaBonté was our next-door neighbor and a farmer. His house and barns were in the village, but the farm about a mile away.

After my first year, 1939-40, at the University of Toronto (Pass Arts, a three-year course), my mother thought I should do something more sophisticated than raking pebbles as my summer occupation. Perhaps she also thought—she never told me this—that remote Jasper was out of the mainstream of recruiting offices. As a fiancée, she had waited four years for my father to come home from the First World War, and he died nine years later, in 1928. A recruiting office was not in the forefront of my mind. True, I was in the militia, as a member of the university's unit in the Canadian Officers' Training Corps, but that was more or less a necessity; it was either the corps or some dreaded form of physical exercise, like running or volleyball. There was no physical exercise in the COTC; we stood around the Armories on University Avenue two evenings a week and in High Park on Saturday afternoons (unless it rained) and waited for our instructors to figure out what to do. By the time they did, it was dismissal hour.

In any case, my mother had arranged Jasper, and I was in an old CNR colonist car headed west. The colonist car was made out of a lot of plank and very little plush. It wasn't comfortable, but it was perfectly serviceable for immigrants and caddies. I had the single upper berth over an old couple who didn't say anything because they were eating all the time, their bags an inexhaustible delicatessen of bread, rolls, sausages and pickles. The couple across the aisle had two babies who slept during the day and cried at night, but they got off at Winnipeg, and an older couple with a daughter about my age took the seat.

The first thing I noticed was that the daughter was wearing a sweater and that she filled it brimmingly.

When she was helping to stow baggage, her sweater was like a blanket with two active puppies playing under it. The second thing I noticed, when I was able to tear my eyes away from her sweater, was the sharp look with which her old man was jabbing me. The girl was a good-looker, too—a longish face, good teeth, bobbed brown hair and an easy smile. She was open and friendly without being forward and gushy. She sat backwards facing her parents, and I sat backwards on my side of the aisle, facing the sausage eaters. I asked them whether they'd like to ride backwards for a change. They kept on chewing. I had to employ a shifty side-long glance to see the bountiful sweater, and every time I did I took a hostile scowl from her father. The mother gave me a polite smile. I took out an old copy of my favorite magazine, *Sky Fighters*, and held it up in front of my face to intercept his scorchers while I peered at the daughter more leisurely. The ploy didn't work because I could feel daddy's eyes boring through the fragile pages of the pulp magazine like two piss-holes in the snow. I finally slid across the wooden seat to the window and watched the green, ripening fields unroll.

Later, the girl suddenly broke the ice. "Would you like to have dinner with us?" Her old man didn't look pleased at all, but the mother chimed in, "I think that would be nice." I trooped into the diner behind them. Papa arranged the seating. He put his daughter beside him and his wife across from her, leaving me to face him on the aisle. No chance of touching even her elbow on a sharp railway curve, let alone any kneesies under the table. I produced my CNR meal chit right away and put it beside my cutlery. I didn't want the old man to think I was going to sponge a meal off him.

The girl's name was Janice and we exchanged all kinds of important information such as the weather, where we came from, subjects at school (I didn't mention I was at university—it was so uncommon in those days that it sounded high-falutin') and where we were going. I said I was going to Jasper to work (I tried to make it seem like I was going to hunt grizzlies; caddying sounded so effete), and when I asked their destination, the old man cut in abruptly, "North." "But I thought it was Grande Prairie," Janice said. "Nothing's worked out yet," he said, glaring at her. He wasn't going to have her tossing out her address to any Tom, Dick or Harry she met. He didn't miss a trick. On the way back to our car, he again put himself between Janice and me, letting his wife struggle with the heavy doors between the cars. There would be no embraces masquerading as saving clutches when the train lurched.

The porter was already making up the bunks in my section and Janice said I could sit with them until he finished and started on their beds. Her old man immediately re-employed his dining car seating plan. A train wreck would be the only chance of ever getting near her.

With the bunks all made up, there was no place for me to sit except in the all-male smoker-washroom. The women retired to the all-female lounge at the other end of the car. The smoke finally drove me from the smoker, where the floor spittoons sloshed their contents back and forth with every bend in the rails. The railroads wanted you in bed and out of the way as soon as the sun went down, and I found that nearly all the heavy green curtains had been drawn across the bunks, including Janice's and her parents'. I fetched the communal ladder and climbed into my upper bunk, hearing the crunching of pickles in the curtained bed below. I was six feet, one-and-a-half inches long and it was a struggle to lie prone and change into my flannel pyjamas. Maybe we'd be able to whisper across the aisle, or hold hands, or (beautiful fantasy) she might invite me over.

I checked the ladder. The porter hadn't taken it away. I didn't need the ladder to get down, but I would need it to get up to her bunk. But I'd have to wait until the coast was clear, whenever that might be. I tried to keep my feverish mind otherwise occupied with a Silent Orth story in *Sky Fighters* ("Eyes glued to the ringsight, knees gripping the stick, his hands darted to the trips of the Vickers)." Then I realized her old man might be able to see my light, so I turned it off and listened to clickety-clack, clickety-clack and thought of Janice with her sweater off. I gave it what I judged to be an hour, eased my curtains apart a crack and squinted out. The car was dark except for the tiny floor lights. The pickle-crunching had stopped and the muffled voices of the last two drinking salesmen in the smoker had died away. There were a few snores, but I couldn't trace the source. "Janice," I whispered. No response. A little louder, "Janice, can you hear me?" The curtains across the aisle from me inched apart. Oh, rapture. I shivered.

The old man stuck his head out. He didn't say anything, but gave me a malevolent wink before pulling the curtains together again. The old bastard. He had ordered Janice into the lower bunk with mama. Well, maybe tomorrow something would develop, I thought. But in the morning Janice's section was empty. "They got off early," the porter told me. End of romance, unrequited.

Jasper Park Lodge in 1940 was (and still is, I guess) a place for the very rich. Why, the individual cottages fronting on Lac Boisvert rented for 100 dollars a day. The menus, like those of a posh club, carried no prices. The staff consisted mainly of students from McGill University (CNR headquarters was Montreal). We were rigorously separated in male and female bunkhouses. Janice's old man would have made a perfect chaperon at one of the female dormitories. There were no female caddies—all the girls were waitresses and chambermaids, roles they never filled at home, of course—so I hardly saw a girl all summer, apart from women guests who were golfers. Except for those on duty, none of the staff was allowed anywhere near either the lodge itself (I never saw the inside of it, and precious little of the outside) or the guest cottages. Even the caddy shack was half-hidden from the first tee—another measure of guest-staff segregation. Caddies had to be summoned to duty by a runner.

I was lucky. On my first day out, I caddied for an old bird in cap and pipe. He was a pretty good golfer and, moreover, paid me two-and-a-half dollars for 18 holes—double the stated fee. I asked him whether I could caddy for him regularly, if he was staying. He said all right. I asked the young assistant pro—none of us dared address the pro himself—how long he thought my old bird would be a guest. "All summer," Vic said. "His name is William D. Mitchell. He comes every year for the whole summer and he plays seven days a week. He was a member of Herbert Hoover's cabinet, the attorney-general, I think." Boy oh boy, two-fifty a day guaranteed every day for seven days a week for ten weeks equalled—my brain worked at high speed—175 less, say, 25 dollars for rainy days or the old codger being sick now and then. But he never got sick, and when it rained he put on rain pants and jacket, the first set I'd ever seen, and turned his pipe over. Only the foulest weather kept him in his cottage, and I used that time to play bridge in the caddy house with a boy named Jacques from Montreal, and two others. Jacques was the best bridge player I ever saw (apart from my mother) and he refused to play for money because, he said, he'd clean us.

I very seldom caddied for anyone except Mr. Mitchell because he didn't start till mid-morning and then played through lunch. We wouldn't finish 18 holes until well past two o'clock. He played deliberately, and said almost nothing. He knew my first name but didn't encourage me to impart any further information. His talk with his playing partners was strictly about the game. I never heard him mention politics or government. One day when we were out on the course alone and silence had reigned for five holes, I timidly ventured to ask him about the senators from Vermont (my home town borders on that state). "Give me the five iron, please, David," he said. And that was that.

He shot a good game and his summer was dedicated to breaking 80. I got caught up in his silent campaign, of course, and defended him against other caddies who found him unsmiling and taciturn. He was easy to caddy for; he didn't hit the ball a great distance, was only rarely in the rough, and he putted well. He often played with the pro when there was no one else around. The pro had a barrel chest and huge wrists and the shortest backswing I've ever seen. He didn't take the club back higher than his belt, but his powerful arms and wrists propelled the ball great distances with surprising accuracy. He couldn't putt worth a damn (he didn't have the patience) and that evened things up for Mr. Mitchell. The pro was always in demand to play because everybody wanted to see his enormous wood shots, so the assistant pro gave nearly all the lessons, though most of the guests were so rich that they had long since bought all the lessons they wanted.

My man, in contrast to the pro, took a full and slow backswing. I thought I could hear his knees and elbows creaking during these wind-ups. He was nearly always straight down the middle. Once in a while he would top his drive and dribble the ball off the tee. He didn't complain, and never had me retrieve the ball for another drive, even when he was playing alone, which was usually the case. He walked the few feet to the ball in front or to the side of the tee and said, "Two iron, please, David."

The summer wore on and my man's score descended little by little. He was seldom worse than 85 or 86, and halfway through August he hit an 81, and then an 80, twice. One day I woke up at the par-four lakeside 16th green when he dropped a long birdie putt and realized that par on the last two holes would give him a 79. "There's a good chance, sir," I said, and he replied gruffly, "Don't say it, it's bad luck, like talking about a no-hitter in the eighth inning." But there was a gleam in his eye.

He was playing with another old bird who didn't talk much, either. My man's drive on the par-four 17th was long and straight down the centre. The ball carried over a little crest and out of sight. His companion had a good tee shot, too, carrying over the same ridge. Mr. Mitchell stopped to relight his pipe and I went ahead, saw the ball when I reached the top of the ridge, and parked the bag and myself beside it, waiting for him to select his iron. He took a six and dropped the ball on the green.

Easy par, I said to myself. I was already thinking of a huge tip for this round of 79. His playing partner was also on the green in two, but away. He was close with his putt and tapped in immediately. Mr. Mitchell was a little strong but came back nicely with a five-footer for his par four. I went to retrieve his ball from the cup and put back the flag.

It wasn't his ball. It was the other guy's. I hadn't checked when I'd come over the ridge and had just assumed the first ball I saw was his. I wished the cup was a hundred feet deep and that I'd fall in it.

"I'll just wash the ball," I said, heading for the scrubber on the 18th tee and hoping, somehow, I could switch the balls. I signalled the other caddy to come quick.

"No, David, don't wash it," Mr. Mitchell said. "That might break my string."

I handed him the ball as nonchalantly as I could, without looking at it or at him. I prayed. But when he leaned over to tee up the ball, he saw. I knew, I just knew, he wouldn't let it pass.

"I'm afraid this isn't my ball," he said to the other golfer. Mr. Mitchell looked stricken.

His companion looked at his. "You're right," he said. "Here you are."

"There's a two-stroke penalty for that," Mr. Mitchell said. "That gives me a six."

"Don't be silly," his companion said. "We're just playing for fun, not even a dime a hole."

"It wouldn't be right. Rules are rules." I knew he would have said the same thing even if he hadn't been attorney-general of the United States.

He would have to shoot an eagle two on the last hole to break 80. So I prayed hard that he would make a bogey five, meaning that even without the disaster on the 17th he still wouldn't have shot 79. He looked weary and drawn. He sagged. But he shot a par four.

"I'm sorry, sir," I said. "It was all my fault." I was nearly crying.

"No, David, it wasn't," he said. "I should have looked, too. See you tomorrow."

He played another five rounds, but didn't do better than 82. He didn't mention the switched balls.

"Maybe next summer," he said when we parted for the last time.

"I hope so, sir."

But my caddying career ended that summer at Jasper and I never saw him again.

Fall had now come, though there had been snow on the surrounding mountains all summer, and it was time to head back east. I decided to hitch-hike part way so that I could visit my cousin John in Hanna, Alberta, where he had a temporary job. He had left his father's farm in Jacksontown, New Brunswick, in 1937, and had kicked around the prairies and British Columbia since, living off jobs that were all short-term and often going hungry between them. One of his jobs had been cleaning out cattle cars on moving freights. Since the age of seven, I had spent many summers on the farm in Jacksontown.

Everything I owned fitted easily into my cardboard suitcase, including my can of clay poultice for drawing boils, and the 82 one-dollar bills I had saved thanks to Mr. Mitchell. First thing Saturday morning I picked up a ride to the Columbia icefield. But it took three chilly hours before I got my next lift, to Banff.

It was only when I got in the 1936 De Soto that I realized fully there was a war on.

"On your way to join up?" was the first question. The driver didn't look too old himself, and he figured out right away what I was thinking.

"Bad heart, or I'd have been in the minute the war started instead of selling men's suits," he said, knocking his chest with a crooked thumb.

"Going home first," I said.

"Then you'll be joining up, eh?" he persisted.

"Sure," I lied.

I couldn't be choosy about rides, especially after waiting for three hours on a road empty of traffic nearly all the time. I'd have to be ready with some standard replies for the self-appointed recruiting officers I was going to encounter across the prairies.

It was dark when we reached Banff. He pulled up in front of a drug store and offered to buy me a sandwich. I took my suitcase with me and put it under my feet at the drug store counter.

"I'll take you on to Calgary if you want to wait an hour or so," he said. "I have a couple of things to do." I didn't figure they were business things at that hour. I said I'd wait, he drove off, and I supposed that would be the last I'd see of him. But he came back in a little more than an hour, smiling contentedly. His bad heart hadn't interfered with one kind of exercise.

We reached Calgary after 1 a.m. and he asked where he could drop me before he went home to "the little woman." I couldn't think of any place so I said the station, where I could check train times.

"I thought you were hitch-hiking all the way to Winnipeg," he said.

"It's just in case," I said.

Actually, it was to sleep. I thanked him for the ride and the sandwich, and he said, "Good luck in the war, sonny." I didn't think much of the "sonny," having turned 19 in August.

I found an empty bench in the CPR station and lay down on my side, half covering my suitcase with my body and gripping the handle hard. I still had my 82 one-dollar bills intact, not having had to break one of them to buy the ham sandwich in Banff.

As soon as it was light, I left the station and began walking east, looking for a good place to seek a ride. Now I found out just how tough it was going to be. Two soldiers heading in my direction overtook me. Just as they did, a car stopped and the driver offered them a lift. I started to follow them into the car. "Not you, buddy," the driver said. "This car's just for servicemen." It was the last car to stop near me all day Sunday. I was pretty discouraged by the afternoon, and damn hungry, and began walking back into Calgary. I went into the station again and learned that in the morning there would be a train north. Near the station I found the Hotel Noble and sat down in the spittoon-littered lobby to wait for a room. Rooms on the outside—that is, with a window —were a dollar and a quarter a night. Rooms on the inside, with transom only, were a dollar. "Room on the outside," the clerk would intone, but none of the three of us waiting stirred. I was third in line and didn't dare give up my place to fetch a sandwich. Three bedraggled couples came down the stairs separately after hedonistic afternoons behind transoms.

I paid with a one-dollar bill and got the third couple's inside room, after a suitable pause to allow the impression that clean sheets were being put on the bed. There was a sink in the room, though no toilet. The sink was brown and encrusted from having been peed in a lot. There were three French safes in the wastepaper basket. A boil on my arm was giving me trouble. There was no hot water in the single tap so I applied a cold poultice to the boil, even though I didn't have much hope it would draw out any pus. When I went out to get something to eat, I was down to 80 one-dollar bills and enough change for a sandwich. I couldn't take my suitcase out with me when I went to the lunch counter because the hotel would rent my room, so I wrapped 40 bills around each ankle and pulled my socks over them as tightly as I could. I didn't put the bills in my pockets because I thought they'd make noticeable bulges for any sharp-eyed mugger.

The first train out in the morning going my way was a milk train with one passenger car. I asked the conductor if he could let me off where the railway crossed a road going east in the general direction of Hanna. He agreed and sold me a ticket for 25 cents. After an hour or so, he came down the car and said, "Here's the place." I stepped down on the gravel beside the train. Just behind the train, a road crossed the track. At least I was out of Calgary.

I soon hitched a ride with a farmer in his truck. He got to the point as fast as the salesman with the tricky heart.

"On your way to join up?"

"I'm trying to make Hanna right now," I replied.

"To join up there?"

"No, I have to see a relative there before I push on east."

"You from the east?"

"Yes."

"Maybe you're going to join up when you get back east," he said, shooting me a glance like a bayonet thrust.

"You bet," I said, to shut him up.

He dropped me at a crossroads and before long a middle-aged man, probably a salesman because he had a lot of boxes in the back seat, picked me up. It didn't take him long to get to it.

"How old are you, son?"

"Nineteen last month."

"Just military age," he said. I twitched the left side of my face to make it appear I was under some terrible stress. (In the winter, I doubled up my right hand inside my overcoat sleeve to fake an amputation.) The twitch didn't fool him for a second. "You look healthy enough," he said.

He stopped at the next village. "If you're still on the road when I finish my business here I'll pick you up again." I tried out my limp when I got out of the car, but he wasn't looking.

I went into the Chinese restaurant. I was the only customer. I was looking at the list of sandwiches when the counterman said, "It's just as cheap if you get the full-course dinner." I had rice soup, sausages, mashed potatoes, carrots, a piece of raisin pie and a glass of milk for 30 cents. The cook-counterman-waiter didn't ask whether I was going to join up. When I left, I couldn't see the salesman's car anywhere so I stood at the end of the village and looked at miles of stubble. The next ride got me to Craigmyle. I sat in the back seat because the farmer had his wife with him.

"Our oldest son is already in England with the army," the woman said. The farmer chimed in right behind, "Which service are you going to try for?"

"The air force, I think," I said limply. With the grain cut, every damn family could devote itself to recruiting full time.

I made Hanna late in the afternoon. Poole Construction Company of Edmonton was putting in Hanna's first water and sewer system and the whole place was dug up. It wasn't difficult to find John because he was the bookkeeper and timekeeper on the project, the best job he'd had in three years on the prairies. He had to look for jobs like that after a bronco rolled on him and smashed his leg at the Calgary Stampede. John conducted me to his boarding house and then to his small room under a sloping roof.

"Just in time for eats," he said, storing my suitcase under his bed. I told him my life's savings were in that suitcase.

"They'll be as safe here as in God's pocket," John said.

We went downstairs and I was introduced to the landlady, a big, sturdy woman named Mrs. Schultz. John and the nine other boarders made room for me at the large round table in the dining room. There was nothing on the table except the cutlery and salt and pepper. Mrs. Schultz waited until everybody was seated (nobody was ever late, John said, and I soon saw why) and then put the food out in the middle of the table. Nobody moved until the last dish appeared. Mrs. Schultz signalled that it was the final one by singing out, "Dig in, folks."

Her command was a starter's gun. Hands and arms flashed across the table in a blinding criss-cross of sliced pork, mashed potatoes, corn, green beans and gravy. The four women boarders asked no quarter and gave none. John began filling my plate as well as his own. "Jaysuz, get in there," he said loudly enough for me to hear him above the clatter of cutlery, which was more like swordplay. I had a fair boarding-house reach and knew how to use it, but I was out of this voracious league. The meat had already vanished off its serving plate and the potato level in the huge bowl had dropped like a Fundy ebb tide. Mrs. Schultz stood looking on, like a referee, but didn't call any penalties. There were no seconds. When the shovelling of food abated, she retreated momentarily, to return with an enormous dish of rice pudding. Again the feverish assault by the boarders. Nobody said a word. There was much sweating, but no time to wipe it away. I managed to spoon a little pile of rice on my plate—without John's help—while remaining seated. Some of the shorter boarders had to stand up to increase their reach to the pudding bowl. The pitcher of milk for the pudding was passed around the table—the only thing passed at the meal—after the bowl was as clean as if a cat had licked it. But no cat would have survived in that house.

"Did you get enough to eat?" the landlady asked me indulgently as she brought in tea and coffee.

"Yes, thank you," I lied. I considered myself lucky to have salvaged a mouthful, and that was thanks to John.

"Wonderful meal, Mrs. Schultz," said a grey-haired man, leaning back, undoing his vest, and picking his teeth with his own silver toothpick. The bank teller, John told me later. He was the senior boarder and acted as a spokesman for the diners after each meal. Only once, John said, had he ever failed to say "wonderful" or "a feast for a king" or something like that; that was the morning they found worms in the porridge. "Can happen anywhere," the teller had soothed a distraught Mrs. Schultz. Those boarders knew when they were well off.

When we got up from the table, I noticed that the old railway clock over the buffet showed the meal had taken eight minutes.

On Wednesday night, John and I went to a dance at Craigmyle. He arranged a date for me with a girl named Betty, and he took Stella, a girl he had known for a few weeks. John had an ancient Hudson (about 1930, I think) and we met the girls in Craigmyle, 10 miles or so west of Hanna. There was no booze at the dance, at least inside, and the music came from a Wurlitzer in the community hall. I shuffled around on my two left feet and hardly stepped on Betty's toes at all. Betty was staying overnight with Stella on a farm near Craigmyle. I dithered as usual and we were almost at the farm before I even tried to get an arm around Betty in the back seat. (The arm was more flexible, too, since the boil had broken the previous day.) It wasn't late but there was no light on in the farmhouse. "Don't make any noise or we'll wake up my parents," Stella said. John parked on the road and we began walking down the lane to the farm. About halfway, Stella said, "Well, we'll leave you here."

"Leave us here?" said John. "The evening's just begun."

"It's just that the dogs will make an awful racket," she said.

"Dogs?"

Just then, two dogs set up a fearful din.

"Oh, darn," she said. "They'll wake up my parents."

"Are they tied?" John asked. He meant the dogs.

"They usually aren't," she said.

John grabbed my arm. He needn't have bothered. I was already set for flight. John didn't mind in the least putting a lead on a bull in the barnyard but, like me, was terrified of dogs, size immaterial.

We could barely hear the girls call "good night" (were they laughing?) as we sped down the lane, stumbling in the dark but somehow keeping upright. We could still hear the dogs as we jumped into the car, making sure the windows were closed.

"I bet she knew I'm scared of dogs," John said morosely. He pulled up the cushion on the back seat and produced two bottles of beer. "Glad I didn't waste it on her," he said. Beer was a luxury. I had had my first only a year before when my city cousin, also John, bought me a draft for 10 cents in a beer parlor in Toronto.

We drank the beers as John drove back towards Hanna. Suddenly, we pitched forward and the car stopped abruptly in the middle of the gravel road. We had been going so slowly that we bumped our heads only mildly. We got out and the two front wheels looked awkward. We didn't have a flashlight. John scratched a match and peered briefly under the front end.

"Jaysuz," he said, "the axle's broke."

I looked towards Hanna. "Well, we don't have far to walk," I said. The lights of Hanna looked a mile or so away.

"It's farther than you think," John said.

"C'mon," I said, "A mile or two is nothing for us."

"Distances look funny on the prairies," John said.

After we'd walked half an hour at a brisk pace, considering the stones we were kicking in the dark, Hanna didn't look a bit closer than when we'd left the derelict car in the road.

"Say, we didn't leave any beer in the car, did we?" I asked.

"I had only the two," John said.

I should have known. John shared everything he had, or, rather, he gave away everything he had and practically never took anything in return.

We reached Hanna about 4 a.m.

"Does your landlady have a dog?" I asked.

"Thank God, no," John said.

The door was unlocked. We took off our dusty shoes and crept up to John's room. As usual, he gave me the narrow bed and slept on his bedroll on the floor.

We got up two hours later for breakfast, duelling our way into the centre of the table to spear the pancakes. John had to be on the job—and had to find someone to tow his car, if it could be towed. I had to be on the road. We parted in the street.

"I wish I could drive you to the next town at least," John said.

"Oh, it's only a mile or so away," I said.

He laughed. We shook hands and I didn't see him again until near the end of the war, when we were both in uniform. I picked up my suitcase with my dollar bills undisturbed. John had paid for everything. "You're my guest," he had kept saying. I was going to miss that boarding house. Eight meals there and not one boarder had asked me when I was going to join up.

But with the first ride, the recruiting drive started again.

"There are some mighty fine regiments right across the west," the driver said. On the way into Regina, another benefactor said, "I'm driving right by the barracks if you want me to drop you off there." That was the subtle approach. Manitobans were especially blunt. "Strapping boy like you should be helping out." And, "When I was your age, I'd been in for two years, right up in the trenches."

It was a relief when I boarded the train in Winnipeg, even though I had to sit up all the way to Toronto and buy sandwiches from the news agent at an exorbitant 35 cents each. Well, I'd soon be back among the other slackers at university. In a couple of weeks, however, I almost wished I was back on those flat prairie roads. I had two part-time night jobs downtown to earn enough to keep me at university, and on COTC evenings at the Armories there was no time to go back to my room to change out of uniform, which bore the flashes of the Canadian Officers' Training Corps. Real soldiers were thick on the streets near taverns, movie houses and restaurants.

"Here comes an officer," one would call out.

"He's real pretty," said another.

"Even after a hard evening of drill," added another.

"Yoo-hoo."

Or they'd be formal, crashing their feet to the pavement and throwing up salutes you could hear twang.

"Evening, sir," one would bellow.

"Your driver will be here in a tick, sir," another would shout.

"Will there be anything else, sir?"

"All tickety-boo, sir."

I longed to be back in that boarding house in Hanna, improving my reach and well away from the nasty world that was beginning to crowd in on me.

Selling the *Star*

There were five of us on the team: Moon Mullins, who was the boss, Steve, Jimmy Giffen, Eddie and me. Jimmy had got me on the team, for which I was grateful because it was the best summer job I ever had.

Jimmy was related to Ralph B. Cowan, circulation manager of the Toronto *Daily Star*. "Don't let him scare you," Jimmy said after arranging for me to see Cowan to apply for a job. I knew what he meant before I got into his office. Behind the closed door, he was talking to somebody on the phone and I could hear every word distinctly. Cowan was the loudest man I ever met, and he used his voice to great effect later on when he became a maverick Liberal Member of Parliament. He didn't shout and he wasn't bombastic; his voice was just loud. His mouth opened wide, but slightly off centre so that you couldn't peer at his palate while he bellowed. He also was a considerate man; he had seen me because he wanted to make sure I really needed the job. Every-body on the team was in the same position, I was to find out.

"Ever sell anything before?" he boomed.

"No," I said.

"Good," he roared. "You won't be telling Mullins how to do his job."

Mullins was nicknamed Moon because every man named Mullins carried that nickname, after the cartoon character of the time. He had been in vaudeville, and had a wondrous gift of funny gab expressed so freshly that it was impossible to tell whether it was spur-of-the-moment or dredged from old stage routines. Movies had throttled vaudeville and Mullins had had to turn his salesman's talents from jokes to goods. For the moment, it was selling three-month subscriptions to the Toronto *Daily Star*.

Steve, like Mullins, was in his early fifties, but a dour man with a small tight mouth who held his cigarettes inside his cupped hand, as if the wind were blowing continuously, indoors and out. He shrugged a lot to cast out the demons of the Depression and to restore images of the great days when he sold stocks and cars and real estate. He had a wife and two children to support. We worked outside Toronto and Steve had to bum rides to the city on weekends. He wouldn't accept a beer because he couldn't afford to buy a round himself.

Like Jimmy and me, Steve usually got a ride on week-ends with Eddie, the only one of us except Mullins to have a car. Eddie had red hair and a narrow, hawkish face that somehow carried a happy smile nearly all the time. He had no responsibility but himself. He spent all his pay, and only when he was broke would he allow us to spring for the gas. He had some relatives in Muskoka, and several times during the summer he took me north with him on weekends, refusing to let me contribute a cent. "You need all that money for college," Eddie would say. "I'll never go to college, so I'll pay." Jimmy and I were the two in college.

Jimmy didn't strive mightily to sell the Toronto *Daily Star* every minute of every day, but he sold enough subscriptions to get by. Mostly, he day-dreamed about his girlfriend. He and I had met in English class. We figured we'd end up in uniform (we did), but neither of us was in any rush. We'd wait for the counter-assault against Hitler.

I don't know how much Mullins was paid as team leader, but Steve, Eddie, Jimmy and I all made the same, 25 dollars a week—which was pretty good for all of us except Steve—plus an extra few dollars if we sold more than our quota of 16 subscriptions in the week. We also received three dollars a day for expenses, and streetcar tickets if we had to go more than a mile. Mullins arranged special rates at the hotels because there were five of us, and consequently a room was usually two dollars a day. At a dollar a day for meals, we could save enough money for a beer now and then without dipping into the basic weekly pay. Eddie was the only one who consistently spent the works. Mullins and Steve needed the money for their families, Jimmy and I for our tuition fees, and Eddie for his car and clothes.

We started east of Toronto in small towns like Napanee and Desoronto, worked our way west to London, and now we were closing out (Jimmy and I, that is; the others kept going) in Hamilton, with a stay of three or four weeks to cover all the territory.

Mullins showed me the ropes on starting day. He knocked on the door of a house on a run-down street and lifted his hat courteously when a woman answered. I stood well back, but within earshot.

"Mr. McIntosh and I" (and he gestured grandly to me) "are out calling this morning on behalf of the Toronto *Daily Star*. We're offering to have the *Star* delivered to your very door for three months at a special price."

"How much is it?" the woman asked.

"Do you have children?" Mullins said.

"Yes."

"They'll love the comics," Mullins said. "We have two full pages of them every day." And he produced a *Star* from under his arm, the pages open at the comics. He showed the woman the two pages of funnies. "That'll keep the kids occupied for quite a while."

"They'll fight over them," she said.

Mullins laughed hugely. "Easily fixed," he breezed. "Just divide the two pages," and he ripped the two apart down the fold.

"I have three children," she said.

"How fortunate you are," Mullins said. "My wife had a serious illness soon after we were married, and she can't have any children."

"I'm sorry," said the woman. I believed him. Why wouldn't she?

"And we have all these women's pages, and recipes." Mullins neatly flipped to those pages.

"Oh, there's a column on sewing," the woman said. "I sew a lot."

"I'll bet you do, with a big family like yours," Mullins said. "When would you like the paper to start?"

"Well, I don't . . ."

"Say, I meant to ask you," Mullins interrupted. "Do you know little Billy down in the next block? He delivers our paper."

"No, I don't believe . . ."

"Well, he has to help support his family, and he gets a good part of the price of the paper." Mullins took out his order book and pen. "You'll like it coming every day," he said. "I'm sure you'll want to keep on after the three months."

She signed the order book. She hadn't even learned the cost of the subscription. It was 18 cents a week, the newsstand price, but it included delivery. Mullins gave her a receipt. "Good morning, madam," he said, doffing his hat again politely. The ceremony had taken four minutes.

"You see," Mullins said to me. "Easy as falling off a log."

"What if she hadn't had any children?" I asked.

"Of course she had children. She damn near fell over some toys answering the door. If she hadn't had any, I'd have gone directly to the women's pages and the big department store ads and maybe features. With some people, you can mention Main Johnson's column on the war, but never refer to the editorial page, except for Les Callan's cartoon. They hear that word editorial and they freeze. Stick to the comics, two full pages. That'll do it nearly every time. Now you give it a try next door."

Mullins stood discreetly at the foot of the steps as I stumbled through a question about how many children the woman had. She had children all right, but they were all boys and all grown up and all serving their country.

"Oh, you'll get the hang of it," Mullins said and drove off, leaving me in the street, forlorn.

But I did get the hang of it before long. I decided to ignore Mullins' advice about Johnson's column on the war after we had been preceded into Deseronto by a Toronto *Telegram* subscription team. The *Tely* concentrated on the war effort even more than the *Star* and seemed to carry a photo of every damn soldier, sailor and airman who joined up—and of their fathers if they'd been in the First World War. The *Tely* wrapped itself in the flag (British) and unwrapped itself only long enough each day to wave it.

"Damn *Tely* war cry," Steve muttered. "They killed us in this town."

I found lying as easy as sin.

"Why aren't you in one of the services?" an elderly man asked sharply.

"I'm only trying to earn enough money to get my mother into a home before I join up," I said.

"Good for you, son," he said. But he didn't sign my order book.

We didn't have to collect any money, luckily. That was left to the paper boy. All we needed was a name, address—and signature. It was part of Mullins' job to call the next day at every address where the team had made a sale, to confirm the subscription. I had only one go bad on me. I was reporting in to Mullins at the end of the day, as we always did, when he said, "Mrs. Burgess over on Oak Street didn't stand up," he said. I thought at first he believed I'd faked it altogether.

"She said she couldn't get you off her verandah until she had signed," Mullins said.

"She did take me a while," I said.

"It's not like you're selling insurance," he said. "You have to know when to give up."

We knew whole areas where to give up quickly: the streets of the well-to-do. If the rich wanted something,

they already had it. It was often a maid who answered
the door, putting on haughty airs with a thin straight
mouth saying primly, not today thank you very much,
and bang went the door. Maids generally acted above
their station—probably their only chance in a life of
servitude.

We swept through the rich districts as fast as we could,
with our calls being little more than perfunctory. Mullins
mapped out everybody's territory the night before, and
each of us had to take his turn on the avenues of the
wealthy. The only advantage was that the streets were
tree-lined and cooler than the bare ones of the poor,
where we prospered.

"The best kind of house to sell," Mullins said, "is when
you rap on the front door and the back door falls off."
His pink cheeks lifted in a huge grin. We clamored to be
assigned such districts. "Please, no more snoots this
week," Steve would say.

Mullins was scrupulously fair assigning territory, and
that precluded any temptation to poach on another
team member's fat (that is, poor) district. Eddie con-
fided to Jimmy and me one day that he thought that
Mullins now and then gave Steve a few more streets of
poor houses than he gave the rest of us because sales
were vital for Steve. Eddie didn't resent this—none of
us did—because Eddie easily had his quota filled by
Wednesday night or Thursday noon, and his efforts for
the rest of the week depended on how much gas he
needed for his car or how much he wanted a new suit.
Eddie could have sold anything to anybody, we figured.
He even sold a few subscriptions in rich neighborhoods, sometimes to the maids, although one of these
sales didn't pan out.

"It took me five minutes just to walk up the driveway," Mullins told our little end-of-day gathering in his room, all but exploding in laughter. "But the lady of the house comes to the door. I guess it's the maid's day off, if they ever get a day off. I showed the lady of the house the order form and she nearly shrieked. 'But that's my maid,' she says. 'Maids can't be having newspaper boys coming here with papers.' She stared at me like I was some cockroach in her kitchen. Then she says, 'If my maid wants to look at a paper she can look at ours after we've finished with it—if it's not needed to wrap garbage—or she can go to the library some time.'"

Mullins slapped his thigh and hooted. "We used to use stuff like that in vaudeville," he said.

Mullins warned us never to go into a house except perhaps just to get the order book in out of the rain so that the householder could sign it legibly.

"You can never tell what'll happen," he said. "The husband might be home, sick, or out of work, or on the night shift. You don't want to give him the idea you're slipping in to fool around with his wife, or daughter, or maid. Maybe he's having the maid himself. I don't want any of my boys beaten up. And if the police were called, think how embarrassing it would be for the *Star*—especially a story in the *Tely*."

I ignored his advice only once. I was working a rich street in London one very hot day, dragging myself from door to door with jacket and tie off, which Mullins frowned on, and hoping nobody was home so that I wouldn't have to go through my listless, fruitless spiel. We were supposed to jot down the house numbers when there was no answer and go back the next day, but in the streets of the well-to-do, we never bothered.

I went up the long walk to a red-brick, turreted house with a deep verandah behind a high, closed railing. A pretty stupid verandah, I thought, with a railing so high you couldn't see the street if you were sitting down. On the other hand, nobody in the street could see any occupants of the white wicker couch and chairs. I knocked, and a voice said from the long wicker couch, "Hello." She was lying down reading. She was a good-looking brunette about my age, in sleeveless blouse and shorts. Her legs were long and tanned.

"I'm just calling on behalf of . . ." I said, going into my routine.

"You must be hot," she interrupted.

I agreed that it was a scorcher.

"Would you like to sit down for a minute?"

I started to sit down on the top step to the verandah.

"Oh, try it over here," she said, pointing to one of the wicker chairs.

I sank gratefully into it, fanning myself with the *Star*, open at a business page, instead of the comics, befitting the ritzy neighborhood.

"How about a cold drink?" she offered.

"That would be great," I said, and she went inside to get it, taking her long, tanned legs with her in front of my chair. She returned in a jiff with a pitcher of lemonade, with ice in it, and two glasses.

"What's your job like?" she asked.

"Okay," I said, "except that I don't sell any subscriptions in a neighborhood like this."

"Why's that?"

"Everybody's rich."

"Do you think I'm rich?"

"You must be. You haven't got a summer job."

"It might be my day off."

"No, your legs are too tanned." That was silly. She might be a lifeguard. But it gave me an excuse to stare directly at her legs. I was also able to peek down her blouse when she poured me some more lemonade. Wow.

"Is this a regular job?" She was full of questions. Learning about how the other half lives, maybe.

"Just for the summer," I said. "Then I go back to college."

"Where?"

"Varsity. Pass Arts. My last year."

"I'm just in my second at Western."

That got us off on a conversation about our courses and campuses, and the time whizzed by. Even if Mullins were driving around checking on me, he couldn't see me behind the high railing.

She was friendly, not snobbish or la-di-da like most rich co-eds.

"Well, I'd better get back to the grind," I said. The afternoon was wearing down.

"If you're around this way tomorrow, drop in for more lemonade," she said.

At the reporting-in session in Mullins' room at the hotel, I said I had a couple of addresses to re-check the next day.

"I thought you were supposed to be in a golden square," he said, using one of his expressions for a wealthy district.

"Yes, but one or two said they'd have to check with their husbands this evening."

Mullins' eyebrows lifted slightly, but he didn't say anything.

"I'm up to 14 already this week so it won't hurt," I said.

I didn't want Tanned Legs to think I'd cadge a meal, so I waited until the afternoon to call. By that time it was raining. She wasn't on the verandah, but I didn't have to knock before she was at the door.

"Come in," she said.

"The verandah is good and dry," I said.

"Oh, come in, I'm not going to bite you." She was wearing a sweater and red shorts.

There was an enormous vestibule and then a living room to the right. "We can sit in here," she said, and indicated a chesterfield in front of a window.

"Did you sell any more subscriptions yesterday?" she asked.

"No, but I told the boss you were a hot prospect and I'd have to come back." I hadn't meant the double entendre, but if she got it she didn't let on.

"I even asked daddy, but he said he wouldn't have that Liberal rag in the house."

"Two pages of comics," I said. "Every day, six days a week."

"That's the social content, I suppose," she said.

"You may be right," I said. "Let's look."

I unfolded my *Star* to the funny pages—I had been showing a war veteran that we carried complete casualty lists and not just those for Ontario—and to my chagrin found that one-and-a-half columns that day were taken up with an Agatha Christie serial, *Sad Cypress*. In the meantime, she had come from her end of the chesterfield to sit beside me. She noticed the large section devoted to the serial.

"You said two full pages," she said. "That's cheating."

"You're right," I said. I went down the comic strips. "Superman. The Lone Ranger. King of the Royal Mounted. Terry and the Pirates. Flash Gordon. Brick Bradford. Little Orphan Annie. All social justice."

"And here's working life," she said. "Tillie the Toiler. Jane Arden. Ella Cinders. Dr. Bobbs. Popeye. Winnie Winkle."

She moved a little closer as we tried to classify the others: Polly and Her Pals, Abbie and Slats, L'il Abner, Napoleon and Uncle Elby, Toots and Casper, Bringing Up Father. She reached across me to point to her favorite, Terry and the Pirates, and I put my arm around her. Mullins' cautionary didn't enter my mind. I pushed publisher Joseph E. Atkinson's Toronto *Daily Star* onto the floor and turned and put my other arm around her and she put her arms around me and we kissed for a long time. She pulled me down on the chesterfield and we went at it hot and heavy. I got my hand under her sweater but when I started to fumble with her shorts, she quickly disengaged her mouth from mine and briskly announced those famous last words: "I don't go all the way."

"Darn," I said. But secretly I was relieved. I'd been spared premature ejaculation on the family chesterfield.

"But this is fun, isn't it?" she said, pulling my head down again. She was right. It beat hell out of rapping on doors in the rain. We went back to the heavy necking, panting and heaving, but not conceiving.

"Rest period," she suddenly proclaimed, as if instructing a workout of the volleyball team. "I'll get the lemonade."

"Where are your parents?" I asked when she came back with lemonade and peanut butter cookies.

"Daddy's at the office and mummy is playing bridge somewhere," she said.

"Don't you have a maid?"

"I asked her not to come into the living room this afternoon."

Pretty soon, we started again. Once when she came up for air she said, "Are you a virgin?"

How could she be so personal?

"Of course not," I lied.

"I bet you are," she said. "Just like me."

"I'll bet you've had more close calls than I've had," I said.

She gave me a hug for that and then, all business-like, said, "Tomorrow afternoon." I thought she was going to write it down in an appointment book: "Heavy necking with paper seller, 2:35 p.m."

I could hardly stand. It was as bad as the time I'd ridden home on my bicycle after a heated session behind the thick hedge on the Butters' property following a school dance. I hobbled back to the hotel and reported to Mullins' room.

"Any luck at that golden address?" he asked.

"Yes," I said.

"Well, let's see your order book."

Distracted, I'd misinterpreted his question.

"Oh, I'm sorry," I said. "I was thinking of another place."

"I think you got filled in instead of your order book," Mullins said.

I never saw Tanned Legs again. I called the next day at the appointed necking hour, but the maid said, "She's playing tennis, but her mother is here if you'd like to speak with her."

"No thanks," I said, skimming down the verandah steps.

A few weeks later, in Hamilton, just off King Street, a woman of about 40 quickly agreed to take the *Star* before I could even start explaining its wonders. She opened the screen door and invited me in. She was wearing a bathing suit.

"No thanks," I said.

"Oh, just come in while I sign," she said.

When I got in, she pulled down one strap of her bathing suit and said, "Help yourself."

I fled.

"You forgot your order book," she called after me.

I had to go back. I kept my foot against the screen door so that she could open it only wide enough to get the book through.

When I regained the safety of the sidewalk, I looked quickly at the book. She hadn't signed.

At the reporting-in that evening, I informed the others that there appeared to be a quick sale at that address as long as certain conditions were met.

"I'd better check this myself," Mullins said.

But Eddie beat him to the house first thing in the morning and returned later with a signed order.

"I think I'll confirm this right now instead of waiting until tomorrow," Mullins said, and was gone.

For the rest of the time in Hamilton, I was assigned the streets of the poor and filled my quota of orders almost as fast as Eddie. I stuck pretty well to the comic pages, though now and then I'd turn to Marie Holmes' Cooking Chat, the listings for radio programs, Ripley's Believe It or Not, or Andy Lytle's Speaking of Sports. I seldom referred to sports in general that summer, the Toronto Maple Leafs being in eighth and last place in the International baseball league.

An old black man one day said to me before I could finish introducing myself, "You send that paper 'round. Yes, sir, you can start today. I want to see that paper." He signed on the spot. I knew he couldn't afford it, but I didn't dissuade him from signing. There were several ill-clothed black children running in and out of the paintless row house. Mullins told me later that he suggested to the old man that he could back out gracefully, but the old man said no, he wanted to read the funnies to all those kids. He paid the carrier the 18 cents the first week, and maybe until he died.

In those days, everybody answered a ring or knock at the door. There were no peepholes in solid doors so that the caller could be carefully examined to determine whether he might try to force his way in. On Mullins' advice, we ignored the signs instructing tradesmen that the entrance for them was at the rear. "We're not tradesmen," Mullins said. "We're businessmen making business calls."

The housewives in the down-and-out neighborhoods had little or nothing and wanted everything shown them by salesmen. They not only signed up for the *Star* but also took the goods of all the other door-to-door salesmen: brushes, kitchen gadgets, magazines, thread, chair coverings, china, pillowslips, handkerchiefs and assorted pots and pans, even the dreaded *Tely*, anything as long as they didn't have to hand over immediate cash. There must have been a lot of fights with husbands in the evening.

A few women would say, "I'd like to, but we can't even afford the local paper."

Once, I said, "But you'll never notice it—it's only 18 cents a week."

"Do you know what 18 cents will buy?" she demanded. I thought quickly: one-and-eight-tenths glasses of draft beer. "Two quarts of milk," she said. I never again suggested that summer that 18 cents was only 18 cents.

Jimmy and I talked a couple of times about the ethics of pushing people to buy something they didn't need and couldn't afford. But we always had those conversations after we'd filled our weekly quota and were working for chocolate bar money.

The *Star* printed its circulation figure every day in bold type on the editorial page. It was above 236,000 at that time, and Jimmy and I scanned the numbers regularly to see what effect we were having on the *Star's* fortunes.

One week circulation was down slightly and Jimmy said to Mullins, "Why are we working like this when other people on the *Star* aren't holding up their end?" He meant the reporters and photographers weren't producing material interesting enough for anybody to read or look at.

"There, there," Mullins said. "There are other factors besides this team, as high-powered as it is. Some people go on vacation in the summer. But it's good to know you have the real interests of your employer at heart."

"That reminds me, what about our vacation?" I said.

"You get yours when you get back to college," Mullins said.

For once, he didn't grin.

On
Guard

My visit to Mimico race track west of Toronto in the summer of 1942 was not to place a bet. The track had been closed, for the duration of the war at least, and my visit was dictated by the Royal Canadian Air Force, which wanted me to help guard the premises.

I had joined the RCAF in April, 1942, for a very simple reason: it enabled me to be graduated from the University of Toronto. My college, Victoria, had brought in a blessed regulation—no doubt in the interests of patriotism rather than of bumping up its number of grads to gain more grants—that, if you enlisted, you didn't have to write your final exams . . . provided you had managed a passing grade that far. I had been so occupied filling my two jobs to keep myself in university that I had neglected to attend any lectures in my last year. It was the recruiting hall for me without a second thought.

I had survived Manning Depot—the collective name given to the horse, cow, sheep and pig palaces of the Canadian National Exhibition—which stabled ten thousand recruits at a time. A little corporal missing three fingers on his right hand—so that he saluted skimpily with his index finger—taught us synchronized marching, and we swung along Lakeshore Boulevard to our own lusty singing of "Hawaiian War Chant."

I had even survived a change in name. My birth certificate says my surname is McIntosh, like that of my father, grandfather and great grandfather in Canada. But when I started school, I switched to MacIntosh so that the Mc wouldn't be pronounced Mick, as if I were some bog Irishman. I was still spelling it Mac when I arrived at the lineup to receive my RCAF identity card as an AC2 (aircraftsman, second class, No. R160129). A male clerk was typing it with two fingers. "Hey," I said, "You've spelled my name M-c instead of M-a-c."

"For Chrissake, shove off," he said. "You're holding up the whole goddam line."

I've been spelling it Mc ever since. My brother still spells his Mac without getting into trouble with the army, the law or National Revenue. Our sister, Mary, insisted on her own embellishment and, until she was married, spelled it Mackintosh.

In the spring of 1942, the RCAF pipeline (that is, us) was so stuffed with would-be aircrew that we had to be hived off into nooks and crannies across the country until there was room at ITS (Initial Training School) to accommodate us in basic ground courses. One of those nooks was Mimico race track.

A leafy lane ran up the west side of the property, and about halfway to the track and grandstand was a small two-storey building used, we assumed, to house jockeys and grooms and other stablehands. There was an office and a dining hall downstairs and, upstairs, narrow bunks for two dozen of us, along with a communal washroom. Our assignment was to guard the old wooden grandstand. There was nothing official on paper, of course—at least that we were shown—but we were told confidentially that underneath the stand were stowed early working models of secret weapons such as revolutionary aircraft and anti-aircraft artillery.

This vital bastion was in the charge of a regular air force sergeant who didn't live on the station (sleeping-out, it was called, presumably at home, though the sergeant never said). He showed up smartly every morning except weekends and some days stayed long enough for lunch. He named three of our group acting corporals without pay, each in charge of a shift of guards, thus excusing himself from practically all duty. About all he ever said was, "I don't want any trouble from you men."

A heavy wire fence with two strands of barbed wire on top ran beside the lane that we took from our guard-house-bunkhouse to the stand. We stood 'round-the-clock guard with two Lee-Enfield rifles that changed hands each time the two-man guard did, which was every two hours. The rifles were never cleaned, but that didn't matter because they were never loaded and nobody had ever seen any cartridges for them. This wise policy prevented any accidents, such as our shooting each other. But the log had to note that the guard going on duty had taken possession of the two rifles from the guard coming off.

On dark nights, it was pretty scary around that big grandstand. It creaked, with or without the help of the wind. I often stood for my whole two hours with my back to a big tree so that, I imagined, no German agent could take me from behind and slit my throat. Our apprehensions didn't cease even after Blackie one night picked one of the locks and, with his flashlight, discovered under the stands broken sulkies and small barrels filled with worn and discarded horseshoes.

I put it to the sergeant that we were guarding trash.

"Nonsense," he said. "That stuff is just to throw any spy off the scent. The real stuff is hidden behind fake walls. And if I find the man who got in under the stands, I'll have him on a charge." He told the three acting unpaid corporals to find the culprit, though he never asked them later whether they had succeeded. "I don't want any trouble from you men," he said.

Our dining hall—three old trestle tables—was provisioned by Crawley and McCracken, the outfit that for generations had fed loggers, miners and railroad builders in northern camps. The cook was a gnarled little man from one of those abandoned camps, and his entire repertoire comprised three dishes: fried eggs, bacon and roast pork. We had either eggs or bacon for breakfast. Both dinner and supper were roast pork and canned tomatoes, the only difference being that the dinner pork was hot and the supper pork cold. The tomatoes were cold at both meals. There was a huge oven at one end of the dining room, behind a wide counter, and the cook kept it filled with pork roasts. In vain we pleaded with him to find another vegetable besides canned tomatoes and another meat besides pork.

"Those things have just the iron you boys need," he would say, wiping the sweat from his face with a dirty dish towel.

"What about an apple or orange sometimes?"

"Oh, you can buy those fancy things for yourselves down at the store," he replied.

Somebody joked one day that Cookie made so few dishes, we must not be getting our allotted supply of saltpetre, the substance the military used to quell, or at least restrain, the sexual urges of the licentious soldiery.

"You'd be surprised where I put it," the cook said.

Saltpetre was always supposed to be in the gravy, but Cookie never made gravy, so we figured it must be in the milk, whereupon milk consumption fell dramatically. Then somebody looked up the word in a dictionary and found that saltpetre was also used as a meat preservative. We concluded that the anti-aphrodisiac was already in the pork when it was delivered to Cookie. I decided to cut down on pork (it wasn't supposed to be safe in summer, anyway), though life at Mimico race track didn't present any opportunities to test the saltpetre level.

But there was an incident which might have provided a test case.

One late afternoon when Norm—my companion on guard—and I were sitting on duty in the shade of the grandstand, our Lee-Enfields lying beside us in the grass, two girls appeared on the other side of the wire fence. We scrambled to our feet and picked up the rifles.

"This is secret military property," I said pompously.

They giggled, and the dark one said, "We're just out for a walk. And we're not on your silly property." I noticed that the top two buttons of her blouse were undone.

"Where are you from?" I asked.

"Oh, over there," she said, gesturing to an area on the north side of the track.

The other girl asked, "Why are you at the race track with those rifles?" She had on a dress you could practically see through.

"We're on guard," Norm said.

"Against what?" she said.

"That's the secret," he said.

"How long have you boys been here?" the first one asked.

"A few weeks," I said.

"We just heard about somebody being here," she said. They looked at each other and giggled again.

"Is there a gate in the fence anywhere?" asked the girl with the see-through dress.

"Nowhere," I said, alarmed.

"Well, I guess all we can do is shake hands," the first girl said, and thrust her arm through the fence. I shook hands gravely with her and Norm shook hands with her friend.

"Maybe we'll see you again," my hand-shaker said. "We take walks nearly every afternoon."

"Oh boy," Norm said.

Back at the bunkhouse, we bragged that we had been making time with two beauties in thin attire. The next day, about the same time, the two girls arrived on the other side of the fence. Norm and I were suddenly joined by three off-duty sentries, and we could see a couple of others almost running up the lane towards us.

"Ooh, how many of you are there?" asked the dark one. She had three buttons undone this time.

"That's a secret," I said.

"You'll probably see all of them before long and you can count them," Norm said.

We two soon were shoved into the background and others took over the conversation, lolling against the fence under the two strands of barbed wire.

The next day, there were about 10 men at the fence when the two girls came along, the dark one in a sweater and the blonde in her see-through again. Norm and I had been completely shut out by this time.

The two girls were close to the wire, and one of the men said, "Give me a kiss." The dark one put her face up to a square opening in the wire and he kissed her on the mouth. Soon everybody was kissing through the wire. Then one man put his hand up under the dark girl's sweater, and she didn't back away immediately.

"Well, we'll be seeing you," the blonde said suddenly, and they were gone.

"Wow," said one of the men. "What a tit."

The girls were back the next day and nearly the whole bunkhouse was present. The acting unpaid corporal on my shift had taken me off the late afternoon beat and put himself on it. But I was there as a spectator of eager lips and hands through the fence. This time the brunette undid her blouse all the way and a dozen arms shot through the mesh. See-Through pulled down one shoulder of her dress so that a breast popped out. But she stayed beyond arm's length and soon the girls sauntered away, adjusting their clothing and giggling.

The dining room at 5 p.m. had a topic of conversation other than the hot weather and which disguise the saltpetre was wearing. By my tally, only two men hadn't yet been at the fence. We thought one was a fruit. The other, Tommy, was 10 years older than the rest of us, that is, in his early 30s, and was married with two children. "You guys must be pretty starved, looking at a tit through a fence," he said.

"Better than that," somebody said. "You can feel it."

"Yeah? I'd better see what's going on." Tommy was one of the acting unpaid corporals.

He joined the milling crowd at the fence the next afternoon, loud whistling heralding the arrival of the girls, right on schedule.

There were no preliminaries this time. The girls came immediately to the fence and began kissing their selections, not just everybody. "Take it off," one man yelled, and the dark one began to pull up her sweater.

Three men started up the wire.

"Get down off there," Tommy shouted. They paused only a second, and two or three others started to climb the fence. The banter had stopped. The men were staring hard at the girls. The girls didn't seem to sense that the mood had changed.

Tommy pushed a couple of us aside and went right up to the fence, only a foot or two from the girls. He shouted at them as loudly as he could, "Fuck off, you cock-teasers."

See-Through opened her mouth to make some retort but looked at the five men on the fence and said nothing. Tommy grabbed the leg of the man who was trying to swing his other leg over the barbed wire. "Don't be a damn fool," he said to the man, who tried to kick free. "Run," Tommy shouted at the girls. "For Chrissake, run."

They ran. But it was a near thing. Two men got over the fence but gave up the chase after a few yards.

There was a lot of muttering.

"Goddam it, Tommy, you're married and get your ass regular. It's not that way for us."

"You crazy bastards," Tommy said. "You want us to be stuck on this damn guard duty for the rest of the war for the sake of a gang piece of ass?"

"They were begging for it," one of the fence-climbers said.

"Maybe, but they didn't want it from twenty of you at the same time," Tommy said. "It's called rape, and they frown on it in Ontario almost as much as they do on drinking beer."

There were a lot of cracks behind Tommy's back about do-gooder and Sir Galahad, but by next day good nature had returned to the camp.

"I bet you just want them for yourself," one man told Tommy at breakfast (a bacon day).

"Already had 'em," Tommy said. "They were looking for a man, not a bunch of boys."

We laughed, but looked furtively at one another. Was he kidding or wasn't he?

The sergeant found out—from the fruit, we figured —but didn't do anything more than utter his usual precautionary: "I don't want any trouble from you men."

Blackie played the major part in the one other incident that might have prevented our getting away from the hated race track.

Blackie was a few years older than the run of us and spent his time off station prowling the beer parlor in the basement of the Royal York Hotel and the corridors of the floors above in search of free drinks and sex. His vast capacity for beer enabled him to have others foot the bill for it by out-drinking them at chug-a-lug. He would hold a glass between his thumb on the rim and his little finger on the bottom, then tip it up and drain the contents. He didn't gulp or even swallow; the beer just ran down his throat, as through an open spigot. For variation, he would hold the rim with his little finger and the bottom with his thumb. Blackie didn't dribble, either, or smack his lips or wipe his neat mouth. He was willing to play the game either way: the most drafts that could be consumed before the beer parlor closed; or the most that could be drunk in a shorter, given time, say 20 minutes. Under the latter rule, he could down 17 or 18 drafts in 20 minutes; his opponent was usually left spluttering and gagging after a dozen or so. Blackie was also quite willing to buy his own round when there were no challengers or when he had run out of them.

Another member of our company was Charlie Burroughs, a puffy-faced youth, decadent before his time, from New Jersey. He said he had escaped the law in the United States and found a haven in the Canadian Air Force. We never found out what he was wanted for unless it was spreading the clap, which he was doing in Canada.

What worried us about Charlie having the clap was that he helped himself to other people's belongings as casually as if they were his own—soap, toothpaste, towels, shaving brush, razor, shirts and, worst, underwear, which he'd take clean and return used, if he returned it at all. We worried that if he didn't leave the clap for us on a toilet seat, he'd park it in our own underwear. We had all had the VD lecture, and seen the VD film, that the clap was spread by sexual intercourse. But nearly all of us believed our mothers that a toilet seat, dirty towel or soiled underwear would serve as well.

One afternoon when Norm and I came off shift, Norm found Charlie helping himself to one of his towels. He confronted him. Charlie said "So what?" and Norm knocked him flat with a hard right to the chops. Charlie crawled under a bunk, and when he came out the other side he was pulling a knife from his pocket. Norm kicked it out of his hand, breaking one of

Charlie's fingers. There was a little click and one-half of the finger folded back on the other. We crowded around to prevent any continuation of the fight, if you could call it that.

"I'm going to report this," Charlie said, holding up his finger with the bone going the wrong way.

"The hell you are," Blackie said, "or you'll have more than a broken finger."

Charlie started to say something but thought better of it.

"Now get down to the hospital and have a splint put on that," Blackie said.

"Where's the hospital?"

"I don't know. Down in town somewhere. Go find it."

"There's no car here."

"Your legs aren't broken."

Charlie came back in a couple of hours, his finger bandaged. "I'll get you for this," he said to Norm. We were afraid he was going to get us all.

When the sergeant arrived the next morning, looking very sharp in his freshly pressed khaki trousers and jacket, he noticed Charlie's taped finger right away because Charlie went to the sergeant's desk and laid it down in front of him.

"How did you do that?" the sergeant asked.

"AC2 Norman Smith kicked me," Charlie said.

"What for?"

"I borrowed his towel for a minute."

The sergeant ordered us all to line up outside, everybody except the two men guarding the secret equipment under the grandstand.

"Did anybody see AC2 Burroughs kicked by AC2 Smith?" he demanded.

Nobody said a word.

"Smith, did you kick Burroughs?"

"I saw what happened," Blackie said.

"I didn't ask you," the sergeant said.

"I thought it would just save time because I was right there," Blackie said.

"Go ahead," the sergeant said.

"I was in the office getting ready to go on duty when Burroughs came in. He was half-cut and stumbling around all over the place. I told him he'd better go upstairs and sleep it off."

The sergeant interrupted. "Where'd he get the booze?"

"I don't know, he must have some hidden around here somewhere," Blackie said.

"This is all a lie," Charlie yelled.

"Shut up," the sergeant said.

Blackie continued. "He tripped on the very first step, put out his hand to save himself, and broke his finger. I even helped to get him to hospital to have it seen to."

"There wasn't any fight?"

"Hell, no," said Blackie. "Norm wasn't even around."

"Smith kicked me when I was lying on the floor," Charlie shouted.

The sergeant said to Blackie, "Why would Burroughs say Smith kicked him?"

"I don't know," Blackie said. "He must have had it in for him. Ask Burroughs."

The sergeant stood in front of Charlie, but he didn't ask him why he had said Norm had kicked him.

"Where do you hide the booze?" he asked.

"There isn't any goddam booze," Charlie said.

"I have an idea where it might be," Blackie said, still standing smartly at attention.

"Show me," the sergeant said.

We remained lined up at attention while the sergeant and Blackie went down the lane. They came back in about five minutes. The sergeant said, "I don't want any more trouble from you men," dismissed the parade and went back into the office. A few minutes later he walked down the lane and was gone for the day.

We crowded around Blackie. "What happened?"

"We found two bottles of beer in a tub of water under some bushes near the stands."

"That dirty Charlie," I said innocently. There was a shout of laughter and I finally twigged.

"You guys owe me two beers," Blackie said. "The sergeant smashed them right there."

We went into the office. One of the acting unpaid corporals was writing in the log.

"What are you putting down?" Blackie asked.

"Just what the sergeant said to put down," he said. "'Inspection parade. All present and accounted for.'"

"That's all?"

"That's it."

"The sergeant doesn't want any trouble, just like he says," Blackie told us. "It might louse up his sleeping-out."

Blackie didn't have to enter any chug-a-lugs to get free beer for the rest of the time we were at Mimico race track. We kept his tub stocked in its new hiding place.

Charlie kept out of everybody's way, but the day we left by truck for Initial Training School at the Eglinton Hunt Club on Avenue Road in Toronto, we made him replace his splint and bandage with a small piece of adhesive tape. We didn't want him drawing attention to himself—and didn't want any more questions.

We all passed the course, except Charlie who vanished about halfway through. We went on to various flying stations and I never saw any of my fellow guards again. Blackie phoned me one time at home long after the war. He said he was coming to Ottawa and would look me up. But he never showed. At least I knew he had survived the war. I didn't know even that about the others.

Minefield

I had arranged to meet Doris in a pub in the Boscombe section of Bournemouth not far from where she lived. She didn't feel confident enough to present me to her family, she said, because her father had a thing about Canadians. Doris said some Canadian slacker had been getting into her mother-to-be's pants (she didn't put it quite that crudely, of course) while her future father had been slogging in the trenches of Flanders in 1917. It had colored his view, not of his fiancée but of Canadians generally.

Bournemouth was the prewar bath-chair capital of Britain. Even in wartime, it didn't appear to have given up this title, judging from the number of oldsters I'd seen being pushed around in their strange conveyances or tottering about on canes, as frail as a house of cards. Many old men wore uniforms, and on the side of one bath chair I saw a gold-lettered name and under it, Somaliland Camel Corps. Perhaps I'd be pushed along the terrace at Quebec City one day, flying the RCAF ensign.

It was here in Bournemouth that the RCAF put its air-crew holding depot for new arrivals from Canada, possibly thinking that the advanced age of the population would reduce our randiness (though they still laced the saltpetre to us just the same). The place would have been a lot more attractive if we'd been allowed to use its long and inviting beach on the English Channel. But it was barbwired to help stop any German invasion, which, by the time I reached Bournemouth in April, 1943, was, thank heaven, becoming a more and more remote possibility.

Most Canadian airmen remained in the depot only a few weeks before being shipped out to an operational training unit. But I had been overlooked somehow in draft after draft, and had become such a denizen of the place that I was placed in charge of an anti-aircraft machine-gun post on the roof of one of the hotels that had been converted into barrack blocks. I never once went up on the roof myself (nine storeys high and the elevators didn't work), but I was assured there was a gun up there. I oversaw the changing of the daylight shifts from a basement cubby hole. There was a German hit-and-run raid on Bournemouth one bright day, but my gunners couldn't get from their sun-tanning positions to the gun in time to fire it.

I explored by bus the inner and outer reaches of the city and found it to be street after street of shoulder-to-shoulder brick houses, clean and quiet. The streets near cliffshore were chock-a-block with hotels which, unlike the big downtown ones taken over for the Canadians, seemed to be occupied mainly by permanent residents, mostly retired.

I had met two or three girls at decorous tea dances. Doris was one of them and attended as volunteer war work, which was what it was considering our loutish dance-floor capabilities. She had black, black hair, merry black eyes and a quick smile. She was no raving beauty but she was easy-going and comfortable to sit with in a pub in the evening. I had already given her two clothing coupons, which is about as gift-giving as one could be in wartime Britain, though a sergeant in my gun crew had bought a peach for 10 shillings for his girlfriend.

I had picked a pub in Boscombe because that section was off the general drinking route of most Canadians. Doris arrived in the saloon bar a few minutes after I'd purchased my opening brown ale. She decided on a small gin and lemon.

"Who's replacing you in the defence of Britain?" she asked. She was aware of my anti-aircraft responsibilities.

"I've had this strange feeling lately," I said, "that the guys supposed to be manning that gun never go up there—that they just report in and then goof off."

"Why don't you go up and look some time?" Doris asked.

"Without an elevator I'd have to be away from the phone too long. I can't take that chance. A warning might come in about an air-raid."

"Then you'd have to go up, I guess," she said. No phone had been installed on the roof.

I told Doris I thought the elevators had been deliberately taken out of service as a partial replacement for PT, the dreaded physical training in which the RCAF indulged. Undershirts and shorts out on a freezing parade square at 6 a.m.—that kind of thing. But all they could do in Bournemouth was to parade us now and then in some remote and seedy street where we couldn't interfere with the bath-chair traffic.

"How is your job going?" I asked. I thought she was a clerk of some kind.

"I inspected rifle barrels today," she said.

"I didn't know you were in the arms trade," I said.

"All of Bournemouth is," she said.

"C'mon. The only industry I've seen is bath-chair repair."

"Well, it's a small arms factory," Doris said firmly. "The seaside resort is the perfect cover. There are small arms shops all over the place. Some are hidden behind expensive shops."

"Like what?" I said.

"Right downtown, for instance, behind that Rolls-Royce showroom."

"What's in there?" I asked.

"Sten guns," she said.

"A great aid to drinking," I said. I told Doris a story I'd heard only a few days before about a Canadian squadron in North Africa. It found itself fortuitously based near a vineyard where there was a huge wooden vat full of wine accessible through a bung-hole on top. Not having any ice cream parlor straws and none in the supply pipeline, they'd sucked up the wine through the barrels of their Sten guns, which were easily disassembled. The only difficulty was that thanks to shaky fingers and loose lips, a lot of their heavy straws dropped into the vat. This pleased the squadron armament officer because the Sten had a bad habit of going off accidentally and killing more friendlies than enemies. The more Sten barrels at the bottom of that vat, the safer.

Doris said I was joking.

"Not at all," I said. "Besides, you're the arms expert —you should know whether you can suck North African wine through a Sten-gun barrel."

"I'll check on my next inspection," she promised, "but it may be a little awkward getting the wine onto the assembly line."

We were tucked into a cosy corner where I could try to play kneesies and look down her dress. By her third gin she was leaning over so I could see better. When I fetched the next round, I told the publican to make hers a double and to put a couple of shots of rum into my brown ale.

"This is a double," Doris said.

"Yes," I confessed.

"Good," she said.

We were just finishing these when a group of oafish Canadians came in, saw Doris and the Canada flash on my shoulder and sat down with us uninvited and unwanted, as if it were a table reserved for Canadians and guests.

"Hi ya, gorgeous," one of the oafs said to Doris.

"We're just leaving," I said. "You guys find your own company."

"Don't be so selfish," a second oaf said.

"Why can't you ever find your own damn pub?" I said petulantly. I had gone to all the trouble to reconnoitre this one and they just stumble on it without a bit of research.

I went into the off-licence part of the pub and bought a small bottle of gin and a large bottle of lemon. I already had two cups, which I nearly always carried with me in the evening. They were collapsible metal cups and came in very useful when harried publicans ran out of glasses in their Canadian-clogged premises.

When we got outside, a little unsteadily, it was still daylight.

"Let's go down to the beach," I said. "I've always wanted to visit an English beach."

"We can't get on it," Doris said.

"We can at least look," I said.

The beach was only a couple of blocks away. We found a little ravine that led down towards the shore and followed it through some bushes until we ran into a barbed-wire fence and "keep out" signs.

"See," said Doris.

We went along the fence a short way till we found a warm little glade.

I produced my two collapsible cups and instructed Doris how to hold hers at the top between thumb and index finger so it wouldn't collapse when it was full. She held both cups adroitly while I poured two gins and splashed in the lemon. I hate gin, but with the lemon and on top of the rum and brown ale, it wasn't bad. I took off my uniform jacket and spread it out for us to sit on. We sipped our drinks, watched the sun drop into the Channel and kissed.

Doris stood up and took her dress off and hung it over a bush. It was just to prevent mussing, she said, and she still had everything else on, not counting her shoes, when she lay down on my jacket, which, clearly, wouldn't cover the prospective field of action. I put the cap on the gin bottle and took my pants off, just to prevent creasing, I said. I still had my issue tie on. We got as comfortable as we could—there seemed to be a little hummock under us—and began kissing again. I felt a delicious little sting on my behind. Wow, where did Doris learn to do things like that?

"Ooh," she gasped. "Where did you learn to do that?"

I didn't know what she was talking about.

"Ouch," she said, "that was too strong." What did she mean? The drink?

I felt a nip, which wasn't as delicious as the little ones that had preceded it.

"Eek," Doris said. Whatever I was supposed to have been doing right she didn't appreciate any more. She pushed me away and sat up.

She gave a little screech and sprang up. I looked down. There were ants all over us. We were doing it, or trying to do it, on a fucking anthill.

She took off her pants, but not for me. It was to make sure she got rid of all the ants in them. I had to remove my shorts and shake them out.

She had little red stings on her thighs. "And I thought it was you," Doris said, and began to laugh.

"I wondered where you'd picked up those sexy tricks," I said. I began to laugh, too.

"I guess we're not up to it," she said.

"Well, I'm not," I said, glancing at my pitiful appendage. More laughter, but I think she laughed a little more gaily than I did.

We put our underwear back on, moved my jacket well away from the anthill, and sat sipping another gin and lemon. It was getting dark, and by the time we finished the bottle it was night, with the moon rising.

"Time for a moonlight swim," I said.

"What about the barbed wire?" she said.

"We can get over or under it," I said confidently.

I pulled up the bottom strand as far as I could and Doris rolled under it in her bra and pants and then held the wire for me. I was surprised that there wasn't more fencing than that, and in a few steps we were on the sand and running for the water. It was shallow a long way out and not really deep enough for swimming. So we sat down in the surf.

"There shouldn't be any ants here," Doris said.

"Then what'll we do for thrills?" I said.

"Rely on ourselves this time," she said. We went into a clinch, lying in the sand.

"Don't move!" The shout came through a bullhorn up on the cliff somewhere.

Another erection evaporated. The long-awaited German invasion must have started.

Another shout. "You're in a minefield."

"Oh, my God," said Doris, taking the words out of my mouth.

A second later, a searchlight snapped on momentarily. It caught us like two moths on a toothpick.

"Some blackout," I said to Doris.

"Don't move!" the bullhorn announced again. "There are mines all around you."

He convinced me. I didn't dare blink for fear I'd set one off.

"My God, what will Dad say?" Doris said.

"Tell him I'm a Canadian and he won't blame you," I said between chattering teeth. How warm it had been only a moment before, and now how cold.

"Well, it was your idea," she said, truthfully but uncharitably.

"Stay where you are," the bullhorn bellowed again. "We're coming after you."

We sat there shivering in the shallow surf, and after 15 minutes or so two soldiers with big flashlights approached slowly. They were consulting some kind of map—an accurate one of the minefield, I hoped.

"Don't move," one soldier said.

"Does shivering count?" I asked.

"You both look blue," he conceded.

"It's the moonlight," Doris said. The soldier kept his light on her a lot longer than necessary.

"I like your swimsuit," the other soldier said to Doris.

"How did you know we were here?" she asked.

"Noise," he said. "You damn near woke the dead up there on the cliff."

"We had a couple of laughs," I said. I didn't tell them what we'd been laughing about.

"We'll have to get a bridge," one soldier said. I could see now that he was a corporal.

"A bridge?" I said.

"Yes. We can't go any farther because we don't know where the mines are beyond where we're standing."

"What about a detector?" I asked.

"It's out on another job. We don't keep one exclusively for swimmers."

One soldier retreated, carefully, and after a while came back with a third. Among them they carried a long bench-like contrivance which, with a rope, they lowered towards Doris and me. I planted it in the sand at my feet. Doris and I would be walking the plank above any mines. It occurred to me that this rescue might be a hoax by three voyeurs masquerading as British soldiers.

Doris went first. She was about halfway across when her contortions to stay upright loosened her bra. She grabbed it to cover herself and stepped off into the sand. I shut my eyes and waited for the ka-boom.

"Never mind your goddam modesty," one soldier shouted, obviously as unnerved as I was.

"I'd rather blow up than have you bastards leering at me," Doris said with considerable spirit. She got back on

the board and stepped smartly across the remaining distance. One of the soldiers gave her his coat.

I thought my shivering would jar me off the board but
I made it without a misstep. Nobody offered me a coat.

Doris and I put our feet in the imprints of the soldiers'
boots and were soon at the barbed-wire fence.

"Our clothes are just down here," I said.

"Not safe," said the soldier holding the map.

"We were all around there," I said.

"There's a huge anthill," Doris said. "Would ants build
a house near mines?"

"My I-card and everything else are in my jacket," I said.

"Okay," he said. "Take the light. But we're not going
with you."

I retrieved the dress from the bush—it was easy to
spot without the light—and all our other clothes, and
returned to Doris and the soldiers. Doris and I got
dressed. She really looked good in that dress.

"Is there really a minefield there?" I asked.

"Take a look," said the soldier with the map, proffering
it to me. It was large and official and stamped "secret" and
showed mines the whole length of Bournemouth beach.

"How did we miss them?" I asked.

"God knows," he said, "unless you're German spies
looking for an opening through the minefield."

He paused. I could see that he liked the idea. Before
he could pursue it, I showed him my I-card. He scruti-
nized it with his flashlight.

"You see?" I said. "Who ever heard of a Canadian
being a spy?"

"Who says you're a Canadian?"

This was getting out of hand.

"Let's go," I said.

"First we have to visit the police station," the corporal said.

"What the hell for?" I demanded.

"To report, what else?" he said. "There has been an incident and an incident has to be reported. Better that or I'll call the MPs." He meant the Military Police, not Members of Parliament. That shut me up.

We made our way slowly up the ravine and along a couple of blocks to the police station. The bobby on duty looked up when we came in and said, "Hello, Doris."

"Hello, Henry," she said.

"What brings you here? This Canadian being obnoxious?"

"No, he's sweet," she said. "These soldiers want to get their names in the paper because they say they rescued us from a minefield."

"Did they?" Henry asked.

"We sure did, mate," the corporal said.

"Dave and I were just out for a stroll and we didn't see any mines," Doris said.

"Who is Henry?" I whispered.

"A friend of my father's," Doris whispered back.

"That's torn it," I said.

The corporal said, "They were down on the bloody beach with most of their clothes off."

"What a story," Doris said.

"We spent an hour or more getting them out of there," the corporal said.

"Was anybody hurt?" asked Henry.

"No," the corporal said.

"Any government property blown up or lost?"

"No."

"Well, let's all go home then," Henry said.

"But . . . " the corporal stammered.

"And thank you for your help," Henry said to the soldiers. "I'm sure Doris and her Canadian appreciate it."

"We certainly do," I said, speaking up, at last. Maybe I should tip them, I thought. All Englishmen liked being tipped. Doris saw me start to reach in my pocket and gave me a quick shake of the head.

The soldiers trooped out, muttering.

"Dad won't hear of this, will he, Henry?" Doris asked. "It would upset him so, to think I had been in any danger."

Henry looked hard at my Canada flashes.

"You're right," he said to Doris. "It would upset him so."

We plunged back into the blackout.

"Hurry," Doris said, "We've just time for a warm-up drink at the pub."

We linked arms and sped down the moonlit street.

Down with Churchill

This was an official visit.

By official I mean a visit undertaken at my mother's command. I was faring no better than my father. When he was overseas in the First World War, he received instructions from his mother and father to visit relatives in Scotland when on leave. In the brief time that had intervened between his war and mine, these relatives had died out and there was no more official connection with Scotland. No matter. Ties of friendship were as strong as those with blood relatives, and my mother kept before me in her weekly letters a short list of old friends who were allegedly dying to see me to get news first-hand from the maternal roof. Very high on this official list was the name of Mrs. Moodie, the childless widow of the doctor in our hometown. She had gone back to England before the war to live with a sister in Bridlington. Dr. and Mrs. Moodie's connections with the church had been very close.

I put off these official visits as long as I could, but excuses such as missing my train connection in London wore thin after a while and I had to face up to a dry weekend in some outlandish corner of Britain.

So I stuffed a change of underwear, shirt and socks and a Simenon into my all-purpose shoulder knapsack one Saturday morning and headed for York. I entertained some idea that even at the last minute I could telephone Mrs. Moodie and say my weekend leave had been suddenly cancelled.

York disabused me of that idea, even though I was unenthusiastic at the prospect of a leave in a little old lady's house where my every move would be noted and reported to my mother in three or four airmail forms, one or two not being enough. Yorkshire was full of bomber bases, especially Canadian bomber bases, and York was overflowing with loud-mouthed compatriots. I did a tour of all the hotels around the central square, hoping especially for the Swan. It had one room hanging right over the sidewalk, so offering a splendid vantage point for propositioning girls passing immediately below in the blackout without running any risk of damage in case they already had male accompaniment. No rooms: the usual story of the war. So I got on a bus and watched the damp green downs and black-and-grey airfields. As we went through the small town of Wetwang, I was disappointed to learn that the name was simply old Norse for wet field.

Mrs. Moodie, uncharacteristically of the English, had given me lucid directions, including a hand-drawn map, to the comfortable brick street she lived on in Bridlington.

"You're just in time for chapel," Mrs. Moodie exclaimed when she opened the door. Every bus I'd ever taken in

Britain had been late, except for that one from York to Bridlington.

Mrs. Moodie, her sister and I sat in the balcony of the church as if we were in the dress circle of a theatre. I sang the hymns lustily, as I had been taught in our village church. I knew all the words, and deliberately shut my hymn book to make sure Mrs. Moodie knew that I knew them. This might provide a favorable line in her report to my mother.

After chapel, we returned to the house, only a few doors away, for tea. There was real food for a change instead of the fish paste served at every air force station I'd been on in England. The scones were light and delicious, not the usual rocks that made a ringing sound on our plates. I told myself I must remember to give Mrs. Moodie the ration coupons we carried for such purposes—it would look a little crass to hand them over at the end of a meal, like paying a bill.

Mrs. Moodie had a million questions about my mother and all the rest of her old friends in Canada. She was a small woman with a snap in her eyes and she perched out at the edge of her hard chair, craning forward not to miss a word of my news. The late Dr. Moodie, in contrast, had been a man of huge bulk. He wore pince-nez and oozed such confidence that when he entered a sick room with booming greeting (doctors made house calls all day long then), you knew the patient was going to get well, and soon.

Mrs. Moodie didn't know, or didn't mind, that my news must have been pretty stale because I hadn't been home for four years except for short visits. "Now, how is Mabel Williamson?" she would ask, and her sister chimed in now and then with "my, my" or "how nice for your mother" or "wasn't that fortunate?"

I was just getting settled into gossipy accounts of the comings and goings of my aunts, figuring I could elaborate each snippet because I had hours of this ahead of me (with breaks for more chapel), when Mrs. Moodie suddenly said, "Now, David, you don't want to sit around all evening with two old sticks-in-the-mud; you must go out."

"No, no," I protested gallantly. "I wouldn't even know where to go."

"We have it all arranged, David. There's a rather nice pub down the street—you know what a pub is, I'm sure—where you can meet some people your own age."

"I'm very comfortable," I said. "Besides, I don't know anybody else in these parts."

"Oh, that's all arranged, too," Mrs. Moodie said. "Someone's going to call for you in a few minutes."

The choirmaster, I speculated.

"They're quite a nice group of young people," she said. "We know some of them. They are all in uniform like you are."

Foppy Royal Air Force officers, I thought.

The bell rang and Mrs. Moodie went to answer. She was back in a moment. "David, I'd like you to meet Myra Cummings. Myra, this is David McIntosh from Canada."

Wow. Myra was a smasher. Not even her women's army uniform could spoil her figure, though it tried hard.

Myra smiled and held out a warm hand.

"Now you have a good time," Mrs. Moodie said. "And here's a key in case you're late."

When we were outside in the blackout, Myra said, "Grab my arm, and I'll lead the way. It's not far."

In the pub, she led me to a corner where four soldiers and two girls, also in uniform, were sitting behind pints of beer or orange squashes. There wasn't an officer in the bunch. Myra introduced me around. I had a little trouble with some of their North England accents, but after a round or two I began to get the hang of them.

They were polite, but did not defer to me as a Canadian, or as an officer. They didn't even let me buy more than my fair share of the drinks, although everybody in Britain knew Canadians were rich, and especially Canadians who were air force officers.

Politics was their subject, and their only subject. I tried a couple of times to divert the talk into more interesting channels, such as the weather, but finally resigned myself to the fact that I was attending a more-or-less regular Saturday night meeting of a leftist cell. They never mentioned bombs, the blackout, lousy food, line-ups (queues, to them) and crowded trains, like everybody else did. They didn't tell dirty stories and there wasn't a hint of sex, a subject which I would have liked to take up with Myra. She warmed only to politics, like the others. I had no recourse but to sip my brown ale, ogle Myra, and listen to politics.

Suddenly, I pricked up my ears. Had I heard right?

"You're right, Ron," one of them said, "the moment the war's over, Churchill will be out on his duff."

"How's that?" I said, dumbfounded.

"I was saying," Ron said, "that come the first election after the war, Churchill will be voted out so fast it'll make all his fine speeches curl up at the corners."

I couldn't believe my ears. "Winston Churchill, the prime minister?"

They nodded solemnly.

"Go on," I said, "you're just trying to kid a colonial Canadian."

"No, no," Ron said. "We're perfectly serious. We can't have that old bastard trying to run the country in peacetime."

I was almost sputtering. "How can you say that? He's done everything for you people."

"Done everything for you people?" Ron echoed. "He doesn't give a damn about the people. He cares about class, about the aristocracy, and how to preserve it. We've taken it too long from the nobs. It's the turn of the ordinary working stiff."

I wondered whether I should fetch a policeman right then and there.

"You're nuts," I said. "Churchill is so popular he'll stay in office until he wants to leave."

"Popular?" Ron said. "See how many votes you'd get for him right now in this pub."

Ron, a neatly dressed private with his cap tucked in under the shoulder strap of his battle dress, had already fought in the western desert; I couldn't very well accuse him of treason. But imagine. Voting Churchill out first chance. What was wrong with these people?

Myra said, "I guess you Canadians like the Empire and being a colony."

"We're not a colony," I protested hotly.

"Well, you're talking like a colonist," she said. The others looked at me with a trace of mockery. Fine friends Mrs. Moodie had picked for me.

Ron eased me out of the hole I was in. "Let's have another round," he said briskly. "Then we'll have some fish and chips."

"Loser pays," I said, partly mollified, getting up to go for more beer. These English political dumbbells weren't going to buy any more rounds for a Canadian college graduate.

We stayed off Churchill the rest of the evening, though their talk about cradle-to-the-grave security, national health insurance and the like baffled me even more. Boy, the limeys were going to be in real trouble after the war if they got into that kind of thing.

Myra sensed that I was a bit out of it and suggested that she and I go to the chip shop up the street and bring back enough for everybody. She started to take up a collection at the table. I offered to pay for the group, but the others wouldn't hear of it.

Myra and I stumbled through the blackout curtain and into the pitch darkness of the sidewalk. I had left my flashlight in my knapsack but she said we didn't need one—she knew the way. We locked arms and kept in step, good protection against the people we bumped into.

"I wonder how many pregnancies are caused by the blackout," I said.

"One less than perhaps you estimated," she said, laughing.

"You really can talk about something besides politics," I said.

"Oh, yes," she said, "when it's absolutely necessary."

We bought two pounds of lard masquerading as fish and chips, wrapped in newspaper, and headed back for the pub. I put my arm around her waist, and she put hers around mine.

"Don't drop the chips," she said.

"I know," I said, "they'd break the sidewalk."

Our return to the pub brought cheers from our corner. I plunked down the ball of fat in the middle of the table and everybody plunged in.

"Time, gentlemen, please," the publican intoned a few minutes later, and we rushed to get a last round. They

were out of brown ale, so I had a mild-and-bitter. I suddenly remembered where I was staying and ordered a
half instead of a pint. The piano was going and it was
pretty noisy, but that didn't deter the political round-
robin at our table. I heard someone's question about
whether there would be a grant for burial when the revolution came.

They all escorted me back to Mrs. Moodie's. We shook
hands all 'round, each of us groping to find the correct
hand belonging to each dim face.

"Down with Churchill," Ron said.

I thanked them for an evening far different from the
one I had expected. I put my arms around Myra and
kissed her beautiful, but cool, lips.

"See you in chapel," she said.

I was fumbling with the key Mrs. Moodie had given
me when the door opened from the other side.

"Well, did you have a nice evening, David?" Mrs.
Moodie asked.

"Yes," I assured her, "but you shouldn't have waited up
for me." I was a little tiddly, but not tight, and tried to
talk sideways so that she couldn't smell the beer.

"I thought you'd enjoy a cup of coffee," she said.

She must have seen my strange look because she
added, "There are three people in England who can
make good coffee. The other two also lived in Canada."

It was good, hot, black and strong. She didn't for a
moment suggest that I needed it for sobering-up purposes. She brought out some fruitcake, too.

"I couldn't," I said politely. "Not after that fish and
chips—if that's what it was." I ate three large slices.

"Your mother would have done this," Mrs. Moodie
said.

"Perhaps," I said, "but not if she'd known I'd been drinking beer."

"Oh, but she would have been relieved about the nice company you were in," she said. Boy, did she know my mother.

"They were nice company," I said, "but a little weird."

"Weird?"

"Yes, they think Churchill will be kicked out of office the moment the war's over."

I waited for her exclamation of disbelief, if not horror. It didn't come.

"Yes," she said.

"Yes?"

"Yes, there's a possibility of that," she said. "He's a hero now, but I don't know about after."

"Up the rebels, you mean?" I said.

"Once in your life, David, it's fun to be on the other side of the fence."

This was even more astonishing than the talk in the pub. How could I ever report to my mother that Mrs. Moodie wouldn't mind seeing Churchill gone when the war ended? It would only confirm that I *had* been drinking.

We talked for another hour or so and then she said, "Well, chapel is fairly early. I have a hot water bottle for your bed."

In fact, she had two ironstone bottles, one for each foot. For the first time since I'd been in England I didn't have to get into a damp, chill bed.

Mrs. Moodie woke me in the morning to a huge breakfast with (again for the first time in England) toast that was hot and not brittle-cold.

I spotted Myra right away at chapel. Who wouldn't have?

"Who's that civvy with her?" I whispered to Mrs. Moodie.

"Her fourteen-year-old brother," she said.

I praised God From Whom All Blessings Flow in a loud voice.

In the street outside, I spoke briefly with Myra. Would I see her again?

"Depends where we are," she said. "You know you can reach me through Mrs. Moodie." Not what I might have wished, but not a refusal.

I packed my knapsack and, without saying anything, left all my ration coupons on the little table in the vestibule. I said goodbye to Mrs. Moodie and her sister. "It's been wonderful," I said. I meant it.

"We'll give each other good reviews in our reports to your mother," Mrs. Moodie said with a smile.

How could she be so wise?

"Come again," she said. "You could even pop over for an afternoon if you're staying in York."

"And miss those hot-water bottles?" I said. "Never."

I gave my mother a glowing report on me (two church attendances in less than 24 hours) as well as on Mrs. Moodie.

Mrs. Moodie died before I could get back, and I never saw Myra again. I have sometimes wondered whether Myra and her friends ever recalled after the war that they had given at least one Canadian the pukka gen (correct information) on Churchill. I never forgot. When I became a reporter on politics years later, I often wished I could ring them all in on a conference call.

Keeping Goal

Canadians have a need to play hockey. They don't even require a puck or a rink. I've played with rubber balls, discarded tennis balls, frozen horsebuns and a butt end sawed off a three-inch maple; I've played on rivers, creeks, ponds and iced barnyards when the only equipment available was skates, pulp magazines for shin guards and two pairs of mittens for heavy gloves.

In the late fall of 1943, as a navigator in the Royal Canadian Air Force, I was in attendance at the Royal Air Force College at Cranwell for a wireless course, which meant being able to transmit and receive Morse code (you know—dit-dit-dit-dah equals the letter v) at 18 words a minute, and to fix the transmitter-receiver if it didn't work, which was most of the time.

There were enough Canadians at the college to form a hockey team, which we did, though rather pointlessly because there was no ice, skates or hockey equipment. But we were bound to play. It was winter, or what passed for winter in England (dampness causing influenza as regularly as clockwork), and in winter Canadians play hockey.

We wrote to PT (Physical Training) at RCAF headquarters in London to arrange a game for us, but it looked after RCAF units only; it didn't have time (or inclination, we figured) to cater to small pockets of Canadians tucked away in remote stations of the Royal Air Force. In the nearest two towns that we patronized with our beer custom, Sleaford and Lincoln, we met scores of other Canadians serving in RAF bomber squadrons. They were getting the same reply from RCAF headquarters that we were hearing at Cranwell. Being attached to the RAF was like being sent to Coventry.

But all our letters must have cumulatively and finally taken effect because one day word came that the RCAF was putting an exhibition hockey team on the road, just like a concert party, to play all Canadian comers up and down Britain. The site for the tournament nearest our station would be King's Lynn, in an armpit of the North Sea called, appropriately, The Wash. Moreover, the exhibition team would carry with it enough equipment to outfit its opponents. We organized a bus for the Cranwell Canadians and made for King's Lynn on the appointed date, picking up two other Canadian air force teams at Woodhall Spa and Coningsby, RAF bomber bases along the way.

I volunteered for goal, saying that I had played for the Black Hawks, which was true, though I didn't mention I was referring not to Chicago but to the Stanstead Black Hawks of my home village in Quebec. We all gaped at the ice in the covered arena at King's Lynn—it was the first any of us had seen since leaving Canada. It was also the first artificial ice I'd ever played on.

We bundled into our assigned dressing room and professionally examined the equipment supplied us. I slapped the goalie's pads with the goalie's stick and pronounced them adequate. There were enough pairs of skates so that we all could get a pretty good fit. There were also RCAF sweaters with a red-white-blue roundel on the front and a number on the back. While I was trying to think what number had been worn by my two goaltending heroes, Wilf Cude of the Canadiens and George Hainesworth of the Leafs, somebody took No. 1, so I took 11, for both of them. Boy, were we going to cream those PT instructors on the exhibition team.

Our opponents didn't look impressive when we skated out for the warm-up. They looked muscle-bound, like all PT instructors do, although some of them skated well enough. We weren't that impressive, either, but we had at least a few good players, including two forwards who had played in a Memorial Cup series. To me, our opponents looked like cream-puffs. They'd do well in the first period, maybe the second as well, but would fade away in the stretch. We were all in good shape because we were young, had to walk or use bicycles all the time to get around, and had been kept lean and hungry on RAF rations. The 15 of us had also stayed out of the bar for two nights running, though it was suspected that two defencemen had slipped into Sleaford for an abbreviated pub crawl. There wasn't a hangover among us, but we were looking forward to one as soon as we dispatched these push-up experts.

We did all right in the first period. They scored a long shot on me (bad bounce on that damn chippy artificial ice, which I wasn't used to, I told my teammates), but one of our defencemen got that back with a blisterer from the blueline. We were robbed a couple of times when their goalie made fluke saves from close in. On one, he was lying on his back and thrust up his arm to ward off his own defenceman, who was falling on him; the shot hit him in the wrist. The second time, he was completely screened and the shot hit him in the chin. We didn't have masks then, and there was quite a bit of blood. They took him off to be stitched up and sent in a substitute, who turned out to be just as lucky, though we didn't make him bleed.

In the second period, the PTs brought on a fresh line. They had used only two lines to our three in the opening period and we figured that made sense because they had to save their strength for the three games they were playing that day. One of the wingers on this new line right away stick-handled around our defence and came in on me from the left, with his centreman. I cut down the angle of the guy with the puck, figuring he was going to pass to the centre. Just as he passed, I went down and slid out smoothly to smother the centreman's shot. The trouble was the pass hadn't gone to the centre. It had gone all the way across to the third man on their line, swooping in so fast I hadn't even seen him there. I was lying on the ice 10 feet away from the goal and there's this son-of-a-bitch of a left wing easing the puck along the ice into an empty net.

Cookie, on our defence, came back and said, "Christ, did you see that?"

"Where the hell were you?" I yelled. I hate being scored on.

"Standing there gawking," Cookie said with a grin.

The next time their hot-shot line came out, I decided to stay upright in the net so I wouldn't be made to look such a fool. They skated so damn fast that our forwards couldn't catch them on the back-check and our defence-men stood rooted like two posts, their sticks swinging forlornly like a broken gate. By God, they wouldn't fool me a second time. I stood there crouched, watching the three of them passing the puck in front of me. I heard something behind me, and their line skated back to their end. I looked around and the puck was in the net. I hadn't seen the shot; I didn't even know which one had taken it.

"I can't stop what I can't see," I told Cookie.

"C'mon, cut out the excuses," he said, still grinning.

Mercifully, the PTs didn't use this line very often, only to spell the others periodically. But whenever they felt like scoring a goal, they did. I stopped them once, but even I knew there was something fishy about it. The right-winger tore in from the side, passed across to the left wing and, when I started to move out, passed it back to the centre. The centre hesitated a second, then shot into my pads. He could have easily passed to the right-winger, who would have had me cold. Cookie confirmed my suspicions.

"They're trying to make you look good," he said. "And it ain't easy," he added.

I felt like hitting Cookie right in the mush with my stick, but he was still grinning. So I complained instead. "Can't you guys stop them coming in just once?"

We managed one more goal, a nice clean one on a passing play, for a total of two. They had 10. That one line of theirs had eight of the 10 and I doubted it had been on the ice more than 10 minutes altogether.

We were dead tired getting out of our pads and taking off our skates. We were all asking one another, "Who in hell are those guys?" We agreed that they hadn't been found at RCAF headquarters in London. I'd never seen any hockey players like that since Aurel Joliat (when I was 10 years old, I had been taken bug-eyed to see the Canadiens play at the Forum in Montreal; tiny Aurel Joliat stick-handled with one hand and fended off the bruisers with the other).

While I was having this happy recollection of Joliat, two members of the PTs' hot-shot line walked into the dressing room with their coach.

"Nice game," one of them said. He wasn't being smart-ass.

"We didn't give you much of a game," Cookie said.

"I'm glad you two weren't on the ice all the time," I said.

"You did okay," one of them lied to me. "I guess you know we have more games to play today, so we have to take it easy."

Their coach cut in. "I'd like you to meet two members of the Kraut Line," he said. "Milt Schmidt and Woody Dumart."

Jaysuz, no wonder they were good, I said to myself. We all sat stunned for a second. Then we laughed and clapped and scrambled to shake hands with Schmidt and Dumart of the Boston Bruins Kraut Line, who, with their teammate Bobby Bauer, had joined the RCAF together in February 1942. Bobby was off doing something else in the service at the time.

We talked hockey with them until they had to leave for their next game. When we gave up our dressing room for their next victims we didn't let on what was in store.

From then on I was able to brag that not only had I played goal for the Black Hawks, but I had also played against Schmidt and Dumart. Still, I will have to outlive all the other participants in and witnesses of that game in King's Lynn before I can say, "Yeah, I played against the Kraut Line. Stopped 'em cold."

A Stop
for Tea

I should have known better than to invite Sid to come with me, but this was another official visit and I thought I could use any help I could get.

My mother had sent me a visit bulletin: the parents of a girl who had visited in our house before the war lived not far from where my squadron was based in southern England. Perhaps—my mother really didn't mean perhaps—I might pay a call on them and find out how they and their daughter were getting along. Yes, yes, she corresponded with the parents, but a face-to-face meeting was so much more satisfactory in gleaning news.

My mother was neither gossip nor busy-body. But she had such widespread interests—two of the subjects she taught at school were mathematics and cooking, for instance—that she was a constant seeker and imparter of information. She conducted a correspondence more voluminous than a prime minister's or movie star's. She had friends and acquaintances on all continents and she kept in faithful and lively touch, not with perfunctory Christmas cards but with long, newsy and opinionated letters. She wrote to me at least once a week—the blue airmail form was a severe restriction for her—and was annoyed when my letters lacked what she considered essential information. I had seen *Mrs. Warren's Profession* in London but had neglected to name the theatre. What was the address in Canada of my commanding officer? Maybe she could write his mother. Was Scott's statue in Edinburgh properly protected against bomb damage? What had Deborah Kerr *worn* in *Heartbreak House*?

At the moment, the nurturing of my mother's world-wide communications network required my attendance upon the Worthingtons at Ringwood, not far north of Christchurch, a neighbor, on the east, of Bournemouth's.

The Worthingtons' daughter, Olivia, had come to Canada in 1937 on one of those student exchanges that were always being run by retired British army majors. My mother had taken her in and shown her around for several days. I remembered Olivia vaguely as a plain, quiet girl who ate her porridge and didn't cause any trouble. Her parents had written my mother to thank her for her kindness to Olivia, and my mother had chalked up another pen-pal.

I didn't see how I could face the Worthingtons alone and persuaded Sid to come with me. He could drive the car (we jointly owned a crumpled Morris), and I would divulge a piece of recently acquired information: the location of a pub in the New Forest (near Ringwood) that often had a stock of scotch. Sid wouldn't drink anything but scotch, and it was always in short supply during the war.

Sid was my pilot on 418 Squadron of the RCAF and we had put in a hard Sunday morning censoring mail.

Well before D-Day, June 6, 1944, and for some weeks after, security was stringent, especially in southern England opposite the Normandy coast where our troops landed. Mail was heavily censored to weed out any reference, no matter how trivial, to military positions, movements and plans. (We could imagine German strategists urgently and anxiously asking their spies: where *is* 418 Squadron?) Squadron officers whom the adjutant could dragoon censored the outgoing squadron mail. The adjutant dumped a bag of unsealed letters, mostly blue forms, on our navigational plotting table in the operations room. We were equipped with razor blades (used) to expunge any offending passages about people, places, equipment, tactics, bad food or any other indication of poor morale. We sat around the table, fished out a letter and read it, or pretended to read it. We all knew how boring they were because we wrote letters just like them. Don't tell them anything at home; they'll only worry.

"Hey, listen to this," Rodney said suddenly and began to read an airwoman's detailed description to a girlfriend of her spread-eagled weekend on a bed in the Strand Palace with a male not her husband.

"Who?" we demanded. Rodney was wetting his lips and stopped reading aloud. "Who is she?"

But Rodney with a dirty smirk quickly sealed the envelope and tossed it to the adjutant, who stamped it "Passed by Censor."

"I must remind you officers and gentlemen that these letters are private," the adjutant said.

We paid no attention because we were frantically searching for letters addressed to other than Mr. and Mrs., whom we took to be parents.

After a while, Sid said, "Here's a good one."

He began to read, "'I thought I'd go crazy.'" We waited in pornographic expectancy.

Sid continued, "'It's a month since he went missing but . . .'"

We looked at one another shamefacedly. The rest of the censors' meeting was conducted in silence. Rodney had the only secret, and he carried it to his grave when he was shot down that night.

Sid and his faithful navigator (me) quit razoring neat little blue rectangular holes in airmail forms and went for a drink in the mess before lunch. I had a brown ale and Sid had nothing because there wasn't any scotch. Sunday lunch was the usual watery Brussels sprouts and unidentifiable fish. We set off for Ringwood, having stolen gas from a squadron truck the night before and with my promise of a secret pub swimming in scotch.

Sid proposed a visit to the pub first.

"I was going to save that for your treat afterwards," I said.

"This is blackmail," Sid said.

"It's a thank-you gift," I said.

"Thank-yous are even nicer in advance," Sid said. "Now navigate me to the White Hart or Horse or Deer or Stallion or whatever it is. I'm still your pilot, on the ground just as much as in the air."

I found the pub (the Red Fawn) without much difficulty. It was closed—open again in the evening.

"Go find out if they have any scotch," Sid commanded in his most authoritative captain-to-crew voice.

"The joint's closed," I pointed out.

"Go 'round to the back, or something," Sid said. "We don't want to have to come back this way if they haven't got any of your thank-you gift."

I found a side door and knocked. It opened almost immediately.

"A Canadian," exclaimed the jolly publican. "We don't get many of you around this way since all the troops went over to France."

"I know you're closed," I said, "but if you have any scotch we'll be back later."

"A bit fussy, aren't you?" he said. "The Canadians I know will drink anything."

"My pilot won't drink anything except scotch," I said.

"Does he, now? Well, he'd better have one right away. I wouldn't want to deny a man of principle."

I went back to the car and summoned Sid.

"Special treat, just like I promised," I said.

He was as surprised as I was at his good fortune. We went inside and the landlord locked the door behind us.

"Mum's the word," he said. I couldn't imagine anyone ever snitching on such a samaritan.

The pub was typically rural England—low ceiling, low benches and large tables for the farmhands, nothing fancy, but ancient, lived-in, good-fellowish. We stood at the bar and the innkeeper poured Sid an enormous scotch. I had my usual brown ale.

"Have one yourself," I said to the publican.

"Thanks very much," he said and poured himself a small brandy.

Sid had the grace not to ask for ice. He knew there was none in England.

"Your health, gentlemen," the landlord said and downed the brandy.

"Do you often have scotch?" Sid asked.

"I manage a bit on weekends," the landlord said. He and Sid got into a long conversation on the merits of various brands. I put more money on the bar and the landlord poured another hefty scotch for Sid and another brandy for himself. I began to look at my watch. I had made arrangements with the Worthingtons to arrive for tea, and we still had to find the place.

"You've been very kind letting us in during off hours," I said to the publican. "We must be off now."

"There's no hurry," Sid said.

"Yes there is," I said.

The publican resolved the dispute by putting another generous amount of scotch into Sid's glass. When we finally left, the landlord said, "Come again next week-end—during hours, if you can."

Sid was a little flushed when we got in the car, but he always carried his booze well. He took the wheel again.

"Well, back to base," he said.

"Hey, you still have your side of the bargain to fill," I said.

"Okay. Navigate away."

The Worthingtons lived in a large house on the edge of town. A big lawn at the back sloped away to flower gardens and hedges. A woman came out to meet us. I stared.

"Olivia, is that you?" I said.

She was in army uniform, taller, and fuller, so to speak, than I remembered, and far from plain, with brown hair and huge brown eyes.

She was shaking my hand but she was looking over my shoulder at Sid.

"Hello, David, who's this?" she said all in one breath.

"My pilot, Sid Seid. Olivia Worthington." She dropped my hand like a dead fish and pressed hers into Sid's. She didn't take it away in a hurry.

As I said, I should have known better. Women went ga-ga over him, not because he was tall, dark and handsome,

which didn't hurt, of course, but because of his bedroom
eyes, male division. As soon as a woman looked at him
she was thinking bed. He was thinking of the same furniture all the time, so he had a natural meeting ground
with nearly every woman he encountered. I had been
well aware of this from the first time I had accompanied
Sid into a mess and women were present. Sooner or
later, and usually sooner, they all gravitated in his direction like iron filings drawn by a magnet. I had brought
him along to charm Mrs. Worthington, not her daughter.

"What a break," I said gallantly to Olivia. "I didn't
know you'd be at home."

"Yes, isn't it fortunate?" she purred, looking directly at
Sid. "I got a weekend pass at the last minute."

"Where are you stationed?" I asked.

"Oh, quite close," she said. I bet she was going to tell
Sid exactly where as soon as she got the chance.

"Mummy and Daddy are in the garden," Olivia said,
leading the way around the house. There was a small
garden there as well as the extensive one at the back of
the estate.

The Worthingtons were about what you'd expect to find
in a well-to-do household in England during the war:
tweedily well dressed, well mannered, complaining half-
jokingly about lack of servants and world travel and a "ter-
ribly austere" ration system. They were drinking gin and
tonic and asked what we'd like. When Sid said scotch,
Mrs. Worthington tinkled a silver bell on the large wrought
-iron table and a maid appeared. I said scotch, too, be--
cause an order for brown ale would have raised eyebrows
and unstated questions about my upbringing.

We ran through the preliminaries about how long we'd
been in England, how we liked it, what type of plane we

were flying, how long the war would last and wasn't Churchill marvellous.

"Now, David, you must tell me all about your mother," Mrs. Worthington said. "We have corresponded such a long time and never met. She was so gracious to Olivia, wasn't she dear?"

"Pardon, Mummy?" Olivia wasn't paying attention except to Sid. I was sitting between Mr. and Mrs. Worthington, and Olivia and Sid were side by side across the table.

"I was saying that Mrs. McIntosh was so lovely to you in Canada."

"Oh, yes, yes," Olivia said.

The moment I started a brief account of my mother's activities Olivia began to look bored, and I knew she wouldn't be with us long.

Sure enough. "Excuse me, Mummy," she said. "Why don't I show Sidney your beautiful garden?" I had just reached the most exciting part—a play-by-play description of how my mother had bid and made two consecutive grand slams at a six-table bridge party.

"Why, yes dear," Mrs. Worthington said distractedly.

In an unseemly flash, Olivia and Sid had disappeared behind a hedge.

I must say that Mrs. Worthington seemed genuinely interested in my family. And when she flagged, Mr. Worthington came in quickly with questions about air force strategy and tactics.

"My, where could those two have got to?" Mrs. Worthington asked nobody in particular.

"Oh, they're probably down in the gazebo," Mr. Worthington said.

"Well, it *is* tea time," Mrs. Worthington said.

"You know how Olivia gets carried away," he said. "David and I will chase them up. We have time for a quick stroll, don't we Mother?"

"Well, just down and back," she said.

Mr. Worthington used his cane as a pointer for his flowerbed lesson. As we came around the last hedge, Olivia and Sid, slightly mussed, were coming from the gazebo. Their tunics were undone, but Mr. Worthington didn't seem to notice. "That rose there," he said to me, "has been bred in England for three hundred years."

"I suppose you've been having a lovely chat with Daddy about the war," Olivia said.

"Yes, lovely," I said, looking at her dewy mouth. I shot Sid a glance that should have dropped him in his tracks. He pretended not to notice, and Mr. Worthington poured him another scotch.

Mrs. Worthington finally got the tea going around with the help of the middle-aged maid who, I noticed, was trying to lean against Sid from any angle she could manage when she passed the scones and jam.

At that point, Sid decided to pitch into the conversation, performing as he was supposed to perform when we struck our bargain, my reservoir of scotch for his well of charm. He talked about London as if he were an architect, about London theatre as if he were a playwright, about British idiosyncrasies, which he found so delightful, and the wonders of his home town, San Francisco. Even I was carried away while not believing a tenth of it.

The only one not apparently charmed was Olivia. She looked like she had when I had discussed my mother's bridge prowess. Finally, when Sid was talking about the very first time he had seen snow (near Sacramento, when he was 10 years old), she interrupted: "That reminds me, I'd like to show Sid the skis I bought for that holiday in Switzerland."

That took a leap of imagination, I thought.

"Why, yes dear, why don't you?" Mrs. Worthington said, bewildered.

"Can you remember where they are?" Mr. Worthington said.

"Oh, yes," she said.

"Maybe David would like to see them, too," Mrs. Worthington said. "Do you ski, David?"

"No, I play hockey," I said, trying to be pleasant but getting close to the brink.

"Olivia purchased those skis for a holiday in 1939 but of course the war interfered," Mr. Worthington said.

"What a shame," I said.

"They are very ordinary skis," Mrs. Worthington said.

I was left alone again with Mummy and Daddy. He informed me how Monty was taking on the heaviest German armor in Normandy so that the lightly opposed Americans could make an end run and trap the Germans.

It was about 20 minutes before Olivia and Sid returned. Her lips were parted and she looked languorous. Soon after, we made our polite goodbyes.

Olivia said, "Now David, you must come again for another nice chat. It has been just so, well, warming." I bet it had been.

"Where were the skis?" I asked Sid when we drove away.

"I never saw them," Sid said. "She said they were in the bedroom closet but we didn't make it past the bed."

"You bastard," I said, more in envy than recrimination.

"She was better in the gazebo," Sid said.

"Great," I said. "Don't spare any details."

"You invited me," Sid said.

"Where is she stationed?" I asked.

"Quite close," Sid said.

He took a turn in the road, which would take us back to the pub with the supply of scotch.

"Hey," I said "we've done that part."

"I need a drink after such a strenuous afternoon," he said.

When we reached the pub, there was still some scotch left.

"Do you have to get every break?" I said.

"There, there," he said, "I entertained the whole family, just as you asked."

Short-Circuit

As my mother's personal ambassador in the United Kingdom, I was not expected to restrict my official calls to her friends and acquaintances. Sometimes she volunteered my services on behalf of friends of her friends. I referred to these attentions as semi-official visits.

Thus, one Sunday afternoon during a leave in London I found myself, unwilling but committed, in Amen Court, one of those little alleys—or what was left of them after the blitz—around St. Paul's Cathedral. They were inhabited mostly by clergymen and sextons and others dedicated to the spiritual and physical maintenance of the great church.

It was a dreary prospect, as much of the great city was, of yawning stone foundations from which the fire-eaten woodwork and other rubble had not only been cleared away but also tidied up as if with hand whisks. I sometimes thought that London would have been more attractive if, instead of these antiseptic ruins, the debris and

clutter had been left piled up to await a vast spring cleaning when the war was over. But the British insisted on
sweeping away the devastation as if it had never occurred.

Part of Amen Court had somehow survived the rain of
bombs on the cathedral and the scores of lesser buildings nestled around it. I came to the last number in the
row. It hadn't been the last house in the street, but now
it was. Beyond its outer naked stone wall were acres of
neat but houseless streets of empty basements.

I knocked at the door of Rev. Henry Tatlock of St.
Paul's. The minister of our church at home had casually
mentioned to my mother one day that he had attended
college in the 1920s with the priest and that they had
become good friends. My mother needed no more
encouragement for a dispatch to her ambassadorial representative. Wouldn't it be nice, she wrote me, if, the
next time I was in London, as I was sure to be soon
because I liked the legitimate stage so much, I paid a
call on Henry, and wouldn't that be a delightful surprise
for Chuck? Chuck was the minister; my mother didn't
stand on ceremony with clergymen, or with anyone else.
She once spied Madeleine Carroll, the actress, alone in a
restaurant and promptly went over and joined her for
lunch. A beautiful, kind and delightful woman, my
mother pronounced.

I had fortified myself at the Chez Moi, an RCAF hangout in Denman Street, before taking the tube from
Piccadilly to Blackfriars and walking up Ludgate Hill to
St. Paul's, allowing time, I thought, to take some of the
edge of the brown ale off my breath. Now here I was,
preparing a delightful surprise for Chuck.

The man who promptly answered the door (we had
exchanged notes and he was expecting me) was tall,

eagle-eyed and mostly bald. He had a warm smile and an even warmer greeting: "Would you care for a sherry? It's very chilly today."

It wasn't brown ale, but considering I had been expecting tea, it wasn't bad, especially for a Sunday afternoon.

"Well, how's Chuck?" he said after settling me into a very comfortable chair in his study.

I told him everything I knew about our minister and his family and especially his kids, who were among the wildest in the village.

"Not surprising," Rev. Tatlock said. "Chuck and I were at Oxford. He was over from Canada on some scholarship or other. We had some high old times."

Hey, hey, I said to myself. Maybe I would be able to turn this visit into a greater surprise for Chuck than my mother had imagined.

"What kind of high old times?" I asked. Right away, I realized I should have tried to be a little more subtle.

"Clergymen play it as close to the vest as gamblers," he said. "I don't think I should give away any of Chuck's cards." He smiled a benign smile and I said to myself, drat, there won't be any juicy bits for my mother about Chuckie.

"Another sherry?" He didn't wait for my answer but sprang from his chair and brought over the bottle.

Just as he finished pouring neatly to the very top of my glass, there was a long and terrible scream from somewhere in the house.

The priest didn't say anything. He returned to his chair, refilled his own glass and said, "How do you think Chuck likes village life after his years in the big city?"

It must have been the radio, I thought. I tried to collect myself to reply coherently and tell him about our village and some of the people in it. He looked quite composed.

I related some anecdotes about the more colorful parishioners of Stanstead Wesleyan United (formerly Methodist) Church and was just getting into stride when that terrible scream came again.

"I was hoping she wouldn't do it again," Rev. Tatlock said simply.

I couldn't say anything. The second scream had jarred my nerves worse than the first one. They were already jangled by flying over Europe with 418 Squadron.

"It was the night St. Paul's was hit," he said.

"Oh," I said.

"The blitz," he said.

"Yes, I understand."

"She wouldn't go to the shelter," he said. "She never did go, not once."

"Your wife?"

He looked blank for a moment. "Yes," he said.

I kicked myself. Whom would he have been talking about for God's sake? The Queen?

"There was fire all around us, as you can guess from the neighborhood," he said, gesturing towards the window and the wide emptiness outside.

"She was upstairs, of all places, and when the cathedral started to burn she began screaming. I felt like screaming myself. I had to drag her downstairs and outside and she kept screaming until a doctor was able to sedate her."

"She wasn't injured?" I said.

"Not even when the windows blew in," he said. "Not a mark—outwardly." He was agitated and took a sip of his sherry. I hadn't touched mine.

"She was in hospital for a long time, but they couldn't do anything for her. Trauma, they said. At last, they thought it might help if she were at home. I couldn't see that because it all happened here, but at least I'd be with her all the time."

"She's still in shock?" I said.

"Yes. There are days when she doesn't scream at all, and then some days only once or twice. And some days, until the doctor comes. If she screams only once when there is a stranger here, I try to pretend momentarily that it didn't happen. I'm sorry you have been disturbed."

"Will she ever get better?"

"They don't know. They don't give me any false hopes. 'Some day, perhaps,' they say. 'Maybe never.' I pray for an end."

"And you keep up your work at St. Paul's all the time?" I asked.

"Oh, yes, I'm gone for only an hour or two at most and the woman next door watches out when I'm not here."

He rose. "And it's time for vespers," he said. I finished my sherry in a gulp and made ready to leave.

"You'll be coming to vespers, of course," he said, that keen eye fixed on me.

"Of course," I said. It had been the thing farthest from my mind.

He took a white surplice from a hall rack and we walked over to St. Paul's together. He took the service in a large basement crypt. I prayed for his wife.

Her scream has always stayed in my head, like a piece of shrapnel. But it has jumped out at me really only twice. The first time was a few weeks later when a German supersonic V-2 rocket hit near our airfield north of London. First there was the crunch when the rocket struck the ground, then the thunder of the rocket's sound catching up with it.

The next time, and I can pin down the date, was Saturday, October 27, 1962. It was at the apex of the Cuban missile crisis when it looked as if there was going to be nuclear war between the United States and Russia.

That Saturday afternoon, I was tending some flowers in my makeshift rock garden behind our house in Ottawa when the air-raid siren on top of the nearby school went off. In a flash, I heard the scream from somewhere upstairs in the home of a Church of England priest in Amen Court.

The siren kept screaming, too. It must be an electrical fault, I said to myself. Why would the Russians want to hit Ottawa? The civil service was already doing enough damage.

But I couldn't go on with my gardening and I couldn't bring myself to go into the house and alarm Jean and our two small boys. Should I bundle them all in the car and take off—but where?

Jean came out of the house. I hadn't moved.

"It's just some dumb short-circuit," I said.

"You're pretty white for a dumb short-circuit."

"Oh, I was reminded of those scary sirens in England during the war, that's all," I lied.

"You think the Russians are coming, don't you?" she said.

"Of course not."

I sat down on the back step and waited, and Jean went into the house. The siren screamed for another five minutes before somebody managed to get it shut off. It was still some time before I could go back to my weeding.

A Call on
Mr. Wells

The Three Villages, as they call themselves, perch as one on the steep banks of the Tomifobia River where it cuts across the Quebec-Vermont border one hundred miles east of Montreal. Reading north to south, they are Stanstead and Rock Island in Quebec, and Derby Line in Vermont. A fourth village, Beebe, straddles the border two miles to the west.

Four miles north of Stanstead is a high hill called Dufferin Heights. It commands a breathtaking view of large segments of the province and two states. On the western horizon, beyond the glisten of Lake Memphremagog, one can see the Green Mountains of Vermont, and to the east the White Mountains of New Hampshire, which stretch almost to the St. Lawrence River.

On Dufferin Heights in the early 1920s, Stanstead Frontier Branch of the Great War Veterans Association —the name is taken from the township of Stanstead, not the village—built a 1914-18 war memorial. It took nearly three years. The fieldstones in it were gathered one by one from surrounding farms. So many people attended the dedication that a grandstand had to be built and some people today remember that, as children, they became lost in the thick crowd.

On a granite tablet—granite is a local industry—set in the eastern face of the cairn is the inscription: "These went and came not again." After the 1939-45 war, another granite tablet was set in the western face: "These also went and came not again." The memorial bears 66 names, an awfully long list for such a small place.

My father, Gordon McIntosh, was president of Stanstead Frontier Branch when he died, aged 35. Every Remembrance Day, my mother, brother, sister and I, in sun or, more usually, rain or snow, went to Dufferin Heights in company with one or two Legion members to place a small wreath at the foot of the cairn. Some Novembers the snow was so deep that we had to leave my mother's Model A Ford partway down the hill and walk the rest of the way.

I came home from overseas just before Christmas in 1944. During my months on squadron in England (my sister reported to me), my mother had peered from the window of her home in Stanstead every stormy night and exclaimed, "I hope David isn't flying tonight." I also found that a friend of mine who had gone into the army would never be back from overseas. He had been killed in Italy.

John Wells had always been a bright light in our village. He was basically an entertainer, smart, cheerful and funny. He also had total recall. You might not think that much of an accomplishment at 16 years of age, but John was a verbatim recaller. Say I had missed the Fred Allen program the night before, which I often did with my mother insisting that the radio remain off until all homework was finished. I had only to ask John, "What was Fred Allen like last night?" and he would recite the entire program. Portland had said this, Mrs. Nussbaum that and Mr. Cassidy the other thing. John even managed some of the accents. Once he inserted the commercials until I said they weren't necessary, unless omitting them threw him off track. John never missed Fred Allen, or any of his other favorite programs, because he was clever enough not to have to do homework.

My mother said, "You will have to go to see John's father." This was between Christmas and New Year's. Family and neighborhood ties were much stronger then than they are now. One did not dismiss a dead friend with a quick visit to the funeral parlor or to the funeral itself. One called personally on the bereaved. One took in the bereaveds' relatives when they arrived from out of town. One brought food and ran errands.

"I hardly know Mr. Wells," I said.

My mother just looked at me. Surely by now she had drilled into me the right thing to do. Appointments were kept on time. Letters were answered within two days. It would be unthinkable for her to skip her turn to have the regular IODE meeting at her house. Spinsters living alone were invited to Sunday dinner. There were rules to life.

"All right," I said.

Mr. Wells was a small, polite man with a hump on his back. He was enormously proud of his straight-backed sons. After returning in the evening from his clerk's job, he would hobble to the hockey rink or baseball diamond if one of his boys was playing. John, like me, was a goaltender.

I walked up Convent Street through the snow to Mr. Wells' house. I knocked on the storm door and Mr. Wells came, leaning on his cane.

"Yes, what do you want?" he said.

"I just wanted to say I was sorry to hear about John," I said.

"He's dead," Mr. Wells said.

"I know," I said. "I'm sorry."

Mr. Wells looked at me, then stood aside so that I could go in. He sat down in a stuffed chair, but as upright as his hump would allow, his cane between his knees. He didn't invite me to sit down, but I did anyway. I decided to keep my coat on, though I'd taken off my rubbers in the porch. I was glad I hadn't worn my uniform.

"What are you doing here?" Mr. Wells said. It was not a question.

"I wanted to say I was sorry about John," I repeated, unable to think of anything else.

"Why isn't John here instead of you?" he said.

"I was just lucky, I guess," I said, fidgetting with my cap.

"Why should you have the luck and not John?"

"I don't know."

"John should be here, not you," Mr. Wells said.

"Yes," I said, though I didn't believe that for a second.

"You don't believe that," he said. "All you boys coming back and showing off and telling about what you did in the war."

I didn't say anything. I didn't know what to say.

"Why should you come back and not John?" Mr. Wells demanded.

"I don't know," I said.

"You're here and John isn't, and there's no reason for it."

"Just luck," I foolishly repeated.

"It isn't luck," Mr. Wells said. "John was in the army and had a lot more dangerous job than you did."

"Yes," I said. At least I believed that.

"That's why you're here and he never will be."

Mr. Wells rested his chin on his hands, which were cupped over the head of the cane, and stared straight at me.

"You've come back and he hasn't," he said.

"Yes," I said, wondering how to get away.

"Is that all you can say?"

"I'm sorry."

"You're not sorry. You're glad you're back and that John isn't."

"I'm not glad that John isn't back," I said.

"Of course," he said. "I'm sorry I said that."

He stood up, and so did I. His hand brushed my sleeve, but we did not shake hands. While I was putting on my rubbers, he went back into the house, leaving the door ajar. I closed it behind me and walked home, almost the length of the village.

"How is Mr. Wells?" my mother asked.

"Angry," I said.

She reflected a moment. "Yes," she said.

"Very angry," I said.

"Yes, David," she said. "I understand."

I went back to Stanstead in 1985 to speak at the November 11 Legion dinner in the Legion hall on Maple Street. I also went to Crystal Lake Cemetery to put a poppy on my father's grave, and I went to Dufferin Heights to place a small evergreen wreath of remembrance. I laid it at the foot of the cairn on the side facing west, under John Wells' name.

Rum and
Strawberries

I never ate so many strawberries in my life.

Every kitchen bar we went into that evening, the fare was the same: a big bowl of strawberries and cream and a glass of black rum, with or without water. I prayed for a piece of strawberry shortcake and a beer, for variety at least. Nothing doing. Strawberries were newly in season; rum was never out of season.

The four-months'-long strike in the Cape Breton coal-fields was recently over and I had come back to Glace Bay, the heart of coal country, to report on how things were settling down. I had spent a good part of the day with Freeman Jenkins, the president of District 26 (the Maritimes) of the United Mine Workers of America, and now he was conducting me on a tour of Glace Bay's kitchen bars, or speakeasies, in I don't know how many miners' kitchens around town. The bars operated quite openly, and the police never disturbed them for the tiny revenue they brought in. These bars were far different from the ordinary blind pig. Food was always served with the rum: sometimes beans and toast, or fresh mackerel, or meat sandwiches. This evening, strawberries were the universal specialty. Perhaps it was a throwback to the old socialist saying: "You don't like strawberries and cream? Come the revolution, you gotta eat strawberries and cream."

We sat in the kitchen, sometimes just the two of us, sometimes with the householder and his wife, sometimes with other customers. Twice we were invited into the parlor, but declined politely. Jenkins told me that the invitations were genuine but that it would be bad form to accept; the kitchen was public, but the parlor was private. It was all decorous in the extreme.

Jenkins was not the first Canadian labor leader I'd been able to talk to informally in such circumstances. But he was the most open—and the most pessimistic, despite the strike his men had just won (more or less—there are no clear-cut or overwhelming victories in such matters) after four very hard months.

I returned to civvy street after the war by taking up the only work I had any glimmer of how to perform, or wanted to do: reporting. In January, 1946, I was hired by the Sherbrooke *Daily Record*, then owned by the rich Bassett family, at 68 dollars a month. I got room and board for 10 dollars a week and had about 25 dollars a month left to throw around on the third daily meal, busfare, cigarettes, beer, girls, and clothes, in that order. There wasn't much left for duds. Three months later, the Canadian Press agency in Montreal agreed to take me on at $27.50 a week, an offer beyond my (and John Bassett's) wildest dreams.

The unions were beginning to stir after wartime years of patriotically forgoing wage increases. Business, which included the press, didn't think much of even modest demands for more money, and the newspapers routinely preceded names of unions with "communist-led" or "communist-backed," which meant the same thing: Red, Red, Red.

The Canadian Seamen's Union tried to strike Great Lakes shipping, and I was sent occasionally to the Montreal waterfront to watch the union merchant seamen and the scabs stone each other between lockside or canal bank and ship. The federal government eventually crushed the union with the RCMP and installed in its place the imported American thug, Hal Banks, and the Seafarers' International Union and wrecked the Canadian merchant fleet.

The United Textile Workers of America in June, 1946, struck Montreal Cottons of Valleyfield, the biggest mill of Dominion Textile Company, the very symbol of the Quebec establishment, whose 3,000 workers included children 14 years old and younger.

Montreal-born Kent Rowley was the Canadian director of the union and, as it turned out, the advance man for the Quebec revolution. On August 13, 1946, he captained one of the bravest battles in Canadian labor history. He led an attack on the fortress-like Valleyfield plant, drove out the company police and scabs and thereby won the strike. I got there from Montreal in time to see the end of the riot.

In a hotel later that heady day, and afterwards, we reporters talked to an always cool, relaxed and collected Rowley, who was wise enough to know that today's union celebration is tomorrow's union wake. His closest ally, Madeleine Parent, was always beside him, except when he was in jail for union activities. (They were later to marry.) Rowley didn't use any of the standard union epithets for Montreal Cottons and similar companies. He talked quietly and rationally about all kinds of labor issues, even when our questioning was deliberately provocative. He was like a tutor, and the session was like a tutorial. Rowley wasn't particularly short or skinny, yet, despite his stubborn will, he had an air of wispiness about him. His glasses and neat moustache seemed to add to this impression. He didn't meet the general conception of a union boss.

But Freeman Jenkins did. He was broad and sturdy and combed his long black hair straight back. As with all miners, his only chance of getting out of the pit (except by death or permanent injury) was a high union job. Born in Glace Bay, he was the youngest man (at 28) to win the presidency of District 26, which, in 1946, counted 13,347 members in Cape Breton, mainland Nova Scotia and New Brunswick. Jenkins was boss of the tough Phalen local in 1941 and led a slowdown that resulted in better working conditions. He was elected union president in 1942 by a landslide and re-elected in 1944 and in 1946, when the term was lengthened to four years. In November, 1946, Jenkins received an overwhelming mandate—7,386 votes to 1,930—to call a strike.

Jenkins could use his fists. One night at Miners' hall, he was being heckled by a miner from the floor. Jenkins finally came down off the platform, strode up to his tormentor, punched him into silence, returned to the platform, leaned out and said, "Anybody else?" There wasn't.

There was another side to Jenkins I was about to discover. He read and studied a great deal more than his union's submissions to the coal companies, town council or royal commissions.

The United Mine Workers had one asset that other unions did not have—its own newspaper, the Glace Bay *Gazette*, a daily since 1905 which the union had bought in 1943. The paper assured the union that its own point of view was being adequately circulated among its members. The *Gazette* never seemed to abuse this unique advantage. Indeed, when the 1947 strike reached the final and crucial negotiating stage, the paper said that it would not comment editorially on the situation lest it risk compromising a settlement.

The *Gazette* operated with a small staff and ancient machinery. It had a Canadian Press franchise and carried world and Canadian news. It concentrated on labor stories, of course, particularly John L. Lewis and his United Mine Workers in the United States. Its main sports coverage was of boxing. It covered the local news not just of Glace Bay, but also of nearby Sydney, with its big steel plant, and the surrounding coal towns, Donkin, New Aberdeen, New Waterford, Dominion, Reserve, Lingan, Sydney Mines, Florence and Little Bras d'Or; Nova Scotia's other coal towns, Inverness, Stellarton, Westville, Thorburn, River Hebert, Joggins and Springhill; and Minto in New Brunswick.

The Sydney coalfield, as it was formally called, extended from Mira Bay southeast of Glace Bay to Kelly's Mountain, in the northwest, a crow-flying distance of some 35 miles. Nearly all the coal seams ran out under the Atlantic so that Cape Breton mining was almost entirely submarine mining, nearly a mile under the ocean floor.

Coal was known in the area as early as 1720; outcrops showed along the seacliffs, and the French came from Louisburg to strip coal from the "French slope," which became part of Glace Bay. Regular mining operations by small companies began in 1858 and out of them Dominion Coal Company was formed in 1893. The company was the enemy. It owned the miners' places of work, their houses and the stores where they bought their groceries. By 1947, however, the miner owned his own small house and his wife shopped where she wished. Glace Bay, an incorporated town since 1901, and its neighbors were drab and dusty, but few towns in Canada in 1947 were showplaces of commerce, housing and public institutions.

Glace Bay's sections of town were known mainly by the names of the collieries located in them: the Hub, East Slope, Number Two, Number Three, Number Eleven, Caledonia and so on. Even the coal seams had individual names: Long Beach, Back Pit, Ferryhouse, Collins, Boutilier.

The miners were an island of loyalty, and not only by occupation. Three-quarters of all the coal miners in Nova Scotia had always lived in the province, virtually all the rest had lived there for at least 10 years. Son followed father into the deeps and any suggestion—I was foolish enough to advance one myself that evening—that another, above-ground occupation might be a good move for some, met with a stare of incomprehension or an accusation akin to trying deliberately to break up a happy family through adultery or kidnapping. The miners had their own representative in Parliament, the eloquent Clarie Gillis, first elected to the House of Commons in 1940 for the Co-operative Commonwealth Federation, forerunner of the New Democratic Party. His parliamentary scorchings of Dominion Coal Company were lessons in passionate invective.

As part of the war effort, miners who were not accepted in the military stayed in the pits to help dig five million tons of coal a year at reduced wages.

Reduced wages! The 1947 strike, which began January 31, was, in the main, for a wage increase of $1.40 a day. The basic daily pay when the strike began was $5.84 and the average wage $6.94. There were only 988 company pensioners, and the average monthly pension was $46.25. In No. 20 colliery, it took 73 minutes on average to reach the coalface five miles out under the ocean, and the last mile had to be walked.

I had been down a Cape Breton mine (No. 1B at Dominion) but, I'm ashamed to say, during an off-shift when the company had thrown stone dust all over the place so that, for the handful of visitors, everything was as spiffy and bright as a new restaurant. Our conductor to the coalface was the Dominion Coal Company manager, Harold Gordon, a big man, soft-spoken, who knew every company mine like the back of his hand. When an accident occurred—and there were appalling accidents nearly all the time—Gordon was always first on the scene to lead the draegermen (rescue squad) below. He was brave and tireless. The miners didn't like him because he represented the hated company, but they respected him.

In the end, it was Gordon and Jenkins and not company and union headquarters in Montreal and Washington who had settled the strike, and the miners had gone back June 12, normally a holiday for them. Their Memorial Day had been marked on that date since 1925, when miner William Davis was killed in a battle between company police and miners. The day was first called Davis Day but later became Memorial Day, standing for all miners killed in the pits. The year 1925 had also marked the last previous general strike against Dominion Coal Company.

There was no violence in the 1947 strike, but the shutdown was so tight that miners had difficulty bootlegging coal to heat their own homes. (Glace Bay, underground, is a rabbit warren of old mine shafts and tunnels.) Union strike relief provided five dollars for a miner and his wife every eight days, with an additional dollar every eight days for each child. Free soup kitchens had been set up and free milk provided to children in school. Contributions to the milk fund by churches and service clubs amounted to 963 dollars during the course of the strike. The union won $1.40 a day more, but 40 cents of the increase was hooked to an increase in productivity.

The first kitchen bar Jenkins and I visited brought a blunt greeting from another customer.

"What did you do in the war, son?" the miner asked me.

"Air force," I said.

His expression said "Yeah?" so I fished out of my pocket my air force discharge button with the silvery little wings, congratulating myself that I still kept it handy, though I no longer wore it. The winter I'd worked for the Sherbrooke *Record* I carefully transferred the button from jacket to overcoat and back again each time I went outdoors and back inside. This practice among veterans waned after several months, and only a few now kept it up.

"Hello, Angus," Jenkins said.

"Got your publicity agent with you, I see," Angus said.

"And so have you—your mouth," Jenkins said. That ended that.

Angus was Angus (Blue) MacDonald, a crotchety and constant thorn in the side of the union brass. The Nova Scotia clans were so prolific that many members carried the same first name as well as surname. Nicknames were therefore imperative. This Angus MacDonald was nicknamed Blue for the blue pockmarks on his nose and cheeks from a powder burn in the mine.

I was no sooner seated at the kitchen table than a cereal bowl of strawberries and cream and a spoon were placed in front of me by a woman who said, "Picked this afternoon." She took a seat by the woodstove where a kettle was on the hob despite the warm July night, and a man put a glass of dark rum beside the berries.

"Looks like the strike is over all right," I said. The woman watched with approval as I dug into the berries. Both they and the rum were delicious.

"We had to have that strike," Jenkins said. "There hadn't been one in over twenty years and the whole atmosphere was clogged up with bitterness. The company's idea of labor-management relations was to organize a bowling league."

"So the air has been cleared?" I asked.

"For now," Jenkins said. He looked morosely into his glass. "But this industry is on the way out, at least in Nova Scotia."

"But you've got over thirteen thousand members, and a wage increase," I said.

"Yeah, a dollar forty a day more, and even the forty cents depends on our production in the next few months."

He lapsed into silence, sipping his drink. Suddenly, he said, "Look, let me tell you a few things. You already know that the mines go way the hell and gone out under the ocean. That may sound romantic, but it takes our men two hours and more just to travel to and from the coalface. All those long tunnels have to be maintained. Most of the coal seams are so narrow, some as narrow as three feet, that it's hard to get machines at them. You can't buy machines to do it—the company has to design and make them here. The costs are killing the industry. We produce just over two tons per man shift. That's the average for the whole Sydney field, maybe two-and-a-quarter tons for each man on each shift. Do you know what the average is right now in American coal mines?"

I allowed that I had no idea.

"Five-and-a-half tons," Jenkins said. "We'll never match that if we bust our asses for the next fifty years. Have you finished your drink? Let's go."

We walked no more than a block and Jenkins rapped at a door. We entered another kitchen, and another bowl of berries and a drink were quickly produced.

"I've just had some berries," I said to the landlord.

"They're special," Jenkins said, signalling me to eat and not give offence.

There were a few other customers and one said to Jenkins, "Freeman, did you ever hear that story about Moose River and Frank Willis?"

Even I knew that Frank Willis of the CBC was celebrated for his marathon radio reporting of the cave-in at the Moose River goldmine on mainland Nova Scotia in 1936. I had heard him myself.

Jenkins shook his head.

"Willis was in a blind pig in New Glasgow," the storyteller related. "It was just after they'd got those men out. Willis had had a few and he was going on and on about Moose River, giving a day-by-day and blow-by-blow account. All of a sudden, a woman yanked open a bedroom door and shouted down the stairs, 'Turn off that goddam radio. I can't stand that Frank Willis for one more minute.'"

We all laughed. Jenkins and I lit cigarettes and leaned back in the wooden chairs. He picked up where he'd left off at the last bar.

"Everything is changing since the war ended," he said. "We dug the coal burned by all those navies and convoys. Now bunkering coal is falling off to nothing. And more ships will soon be oil-fired. Just another nail in our coffin."

He put his elbows on the table and his large chin in his hands.

"I went down 1B a little while ago," I said. "It's a long way out."

"Dig any coal?"

"It was a show tour," I said.

"But you saw the seam?"

"Oh, yes," I said.

"You can imagine what it's like trying to dig coal out of a place like that for eight hours."

"It's the ocean that worried me," I said, "whether she'd come through on us."

"There's nothing safe down there," Jenkins said. "The seams are gassy, and the roofs are weak and the equipment breaks down. I remember when I was a boy and the accidents we had then. One time a trip broke loose on the slope and went down like an express train. When she jumped the track, the men in the trip had their limbs chopped off on the walls, like sausages."

"There hasn't been a bad accident for a while," I said.

"They're all bad," he said, "but I know what you mean. There hasn't been a big one lately, but there will be. In the meantime, our men are still getting killed regularly, one or two at a time. Little bumps, they're called, but you're just as dead as in a big bump."

We finished our drinks and Jenkins said, "Let's try another place. Maybe there's a fiddler there."

They must have known we were coming because the rum and strawberries were already set out on the oil-cloth-covered table. There were three or four miners sitting around the kitchen and they all greeted Jenkins warmly: he was obviously an admired leader. He introduced me around, as usual, never missing a name.

"Give us a tune, Gerry," he said.

"You bet," Gerry said, taking down a fiddle from a shelf. "There should be music now that we're all back working."

"Yeah," Jenkins said.

Gerry played "Red Rover" and we all joined in the chorus. I didn't know the words at first but mouthed them until I finally picked them up on the seventh or eighth chorus. Jenkins sang along but his heart wasn't in it. My heart wasn't in the strawberries, but I got them down, one at a time. The strong rum made a good strawberry chaser.

A couple more songs, and we moved down the street again. The houses were small. Some had picket fences, but the combination of coal dust and salt air didn't allow longevity to paint or grass.

The next bootlegger and wife sat with us at the table.

"Freeman, how can I keep my boy out of the pits?" she asked out of the blue.

"Hazel, please keep me out of your family arguments," Jenkins said. "Nobody has ever figured that one out."

"C'mon, Freeman, you've got some idea. You've got kids. Will there be any work five years from now?"

"That's a different question," he said. "Yes, there'll be work five years from now, but I don't know how much or how long it will last after that. You read the papers, too. Oil and gas is the coming fuel, and they're even talking about atomic energy. The company won't be able to sell all the coal we dig. There'll be idle time in some pits and maybe some will close. And anyway, we're too far from the big cities of Canada even if they still wanted coal for their houses and industries. Even the railroads are giving up coal."

"You're saying my son should try something else," Hazel said.

"Hazel, you know as well as I do he can't do that unless he goes away," Jenkins said. "And he's probably like all miners' sons. He won't go away. He'll want to go down the pit with Dad the moment he's old enough."

"Yes," she said. Her husband didn't say anything. She looked sharply at him and asked, "What parent wants her child working in a wobbly tunnel five miles out under the ocean?"

They were all trapped, I thought, trapped in their dangerous occupation, trapped by the company, but trapped most of all by their pride in and loyalty to a calling and to their fellows. I was getting tight.

"I imagine, Hazel," Jenkins said, "that we'll all go down together, like the *Titanic*. The lifeboats will take only the company directors and ledger-keepers."

"You're too depressing," she said. "What did we strike for?"

"A dollar forty a day," Jenkins said. "We won, didn't we, so live it up."

"Whoopee," she said.

"That's the spirit," Jenkins said and managed a rare grin. He squeezed Hazel's shoulder and clapped her husband on the back and we were off up the street again. I had trouble navigating, and Jenkins, apparently cold sober, grabbed my arm to steady me.

"How about some more strawberries?" he said. "I hear this is a great season for them."

There was quite a gang in the next kitchen. I was no sooner at the table, introduced to a variety of Anguses, Johns and Bobs, with a dish of berries in front of me, than a man at the end of the table suddenly got to his feet.

"Excuse me a second," he said, not slurring a word, and went outside. We could clearly hear him retching his guts out. A moment later he returned, refreshed, resumed his seat, picked up his rum, took a long swig and asked, "What's that you were saying, Freeman?"

My reddish eyes popped in admiration. Nobody else in the room paid the slightest attention.

"I wasn't saying anything, but I will," Jenkins said. "And that is, that it's the ordinary Canadian who's going to kill us, and before long."

Everybody waited for him to go on.

"The consumer thinks coal is old-fashioned and dirty. And that means pretty soon he'll start thinking we're old-fashioned and dirty. He won't give a damn about coal and he won't give a damn either about the people who depend on it for a living. He'll want oil, and he'll get oil."

There was a long silence. I guess they all knew in their hearts that what Jenkins was saying was the way it was going to turn out.

The landlord broke the spell. "How about one on the house?" he sang out.

That raised cheers, including mine, though I hadn't paid for a drink all night; Jenkins wouldn't stand for it. The landlord went around the kitchen filling all the glasses from a large pitcher of rum.

"You haven't finished your strawberries," Jenkins said to me. "I'll join you," he added and asked the landlord for some.

"I'm sorry, Freeman, but your guest got the last of them."

"Have mine," I said, pushing the bowl in front of Jenkins.

"Wouldn't think of it," he said, pushing it back. "You know what I've tried? Strawberries with rum. Delicious."

I took his advice and poured my rum over the berries. He was right. A little sweet, but a nice combination.

"I have one more question," I said. I hadn't asked one all evening that I could remember.

"Shoot."

"What do you do when you're no longer president of the union?"

"Back down the pit," he said. "It won't be easy after all the daylight of the last few years, but I'll get back in the swing."

Jenkins was re-elected president by acclamation in 1950 but was narrowly defeated in 1954. He went back down the mine, as an inspector. Later, he became chairman of the board of directors of Glace Bay General Hospital, and in the 1970s he fought off two attempts by the Nova Scotia government to close the hospital. He died in 1979 at age 66.

The union outlasted Dominion Coal Company. The mines were taken over by the Cape Breton Development Corporation in the 1960s, and the last Dominion colliery—old 1B—closed in 1984. A handful of other coalmines are still operating, however, giving employment to some 2,500 miners in and near Glace Bay. They are represented by the United Mine Workers.

The union treasury was exhausted by the 1947 strike and the *Gazette* had to be sold to a group of employees in 1948. It folded the following year.

Jenkins' economic predictions that strawberry-soaked evening in 1947 came true faster than he thought they would. In 1950, I visited the Leduc oilfield in Alberta to report on growing exploration and production.

In the booth of a restaurant in Devon, not far from Edmonton, I found at my knee a peculiar tall shelf built under the table. It was for your bootleg bottle. I asked, but they didn't have any fresh strawberries.

Redfeet

The ferry *Abegweit*—it is always called *Abegweit* because the name stands for (in Micmac Indian) Prince Edward Island—berthed gently at Borden, and most of the passengers, carrying their luggage, boarded the waiting dockside train for Charlottetown. There weren't many of us, mostly salesmen on their appointed rounds, in late November.

It was dark when the train arrived in Charlottetown an hour or so later. It was raw and blustery—peevish, they say on the island—but there hadn't been any snow yet. Several of the train passengers reached the Charlottetown Hotel about the same time. Inside the front door, a pleasant man stuck out his hand and said to me, "Good evening. My name is Gordon Foster. I'm the manager and I hope you enjoy your stay."

A hotel manager who met his guests at the door? It was my first visit, but Mr. Foster greeted me as cordially as he welcomed my travelling companions, who had been stopping at the Charlottetown for years.

"He always meets the boat train," a fellow guest told me while we were signing in. "I think it's why I keep coming back here, though I'm told the food is better at the Queen's." (An acquaintance of mine, Cec Burke, who had sailed with Angus Walters in *Bluenose*, always stayed at the Queen's because he could start his day as he did at home, with a breakfast of smoked herring.)

Next morning, I started my political scouting with calls at Liberal and Conservative party headquarters and at the two daily newspapers, the *Guardian* and the *Patriot*. There wasn't a great deal of excitement about the provincial election, less than a week away, because the Liberals were considered a shoo-in, which is the way it worked out.

The premier, J. Walter Jones, was going "up west" to Tignish for a political meeting and I was asked by the Liberals if I'd like to go along. Sure. A couple of nights later I'd cover the Conservative leader's Friday night rally in town, and that would be that, both sides done up brown and only the results to worry about election day.

With these basics out of the way, my next project was acquisition of a bottle of rum. I'd heard about Prince Edward Island's wonderful liquor laws; now to test them.

In 1947, you still needed a doctor's prescription to buy a bottle of booze at the liquor store. The prescription was called scrip. Some doctors sold scrip on the side. Some found it a hindrance in their practice and wouldn't be bothered. Still others made out the scrip for fear that if they didn't, their patients would run the hazards of illegal moonshine.

I asked Cal Lewis, a small, craggy veteran reporter on the *Guardian*, which doctor's office was handiest.

"This is 1947," he said. "We don't bother the doctors any more. The prescription form is right in the liquor store."

Sure enough. There was a place for a doctor to sign that the patient (me) needed the alcohol for medicinal purposes, and a place for me to sign as the purchaser.

The liquor store was crowded. You couldn't pull what you wanted off a shelf, of course, but had to hand your scrip and money to a clerk who plunged into a hidden stockroom to retrieve the appropriate bottle. I had expected a resident doctor in the store to sign my scrip, but I didn't see anybody with a stethoscope or giving any other indication of medical professionalism. The signers around me were filling in the blank spaces for signatures without the slightest hesitation. What the hell, I thought, let's give it a whirl. In the place for the doctor's signature I filled in D. McIntosh, M.D., and in the place for mine I wrote D. McIntosh.

I handed the scrip and my money to a clerk. He put a tick on it with a pencil he kept behind his ear and went back to the storeroom for the bottle of rum. When he handed me the bottle, I said, "I guess you people never look at the signatures."

"Sure we do. Good to see you, Doc."

And he gave me a huge wink out of a straight face.

"Next," he said.

When I told Cal later about my doctor-patient relationship, he said, "Islanders aren't usually so brazen to use the same name. That would give our law a bad name and upset the Temperance Society. We usually just make up any old name for the doctor. Sometimes we even use a doctor's real name."

The premier, island-born and -bred, was a burly man who didn't look anywhere near his 69 years. He knew scientific as well as everyday agriculture and had written the definitive book on fox-farming. He asked me if I'd mind riding in the front with the driver because he had his speech and other work to go over with his secretary in the back seat. Off we went, half the length of the island, to Tignish in the far western corner on North Cape, nearly 90 miles, through Springvale, Hunter River, Kensington, St. Eleanors, Miscouche, Mount Pleasant, Carleton and Bloomfield. It was dusk when we started and I watched the farms and bays go by as long as light remained. The field work was nearly over for the year and the land lay wet and lonely, farmhouse lamps and barn lanterns puncturing the murk sporadically. A few people were banking their houses with seaweed, earth or sawdust against the coming winter.

The hall was packed with farmers and fishermen and some wives, and the man who introduced Mr. Jones said, "He cared enough to come all this way." The premier's speech was routine, but not perfunctory. He told only one joke, about islanders' longevity. He had met an 80-year-old man, dressed to the nines, who told him he was on his way to attend his father's wedding. He assured Jones that his father wanted to get married—it wasn't a shotgun wedding. (The premier told this joke several years later at a state dinner for Queen Elizabeth II. The Queen smiled thinly.)

The premier got a good hand, we all got a lobster sandwich and coffee and then we started back for Charlottetown. I remained in the front seat.

Mr. Jones said to me, "What did you think of the meeting?"

"The thing I noticed most is that Prince Edward Island is red—not speaking politically," I said. "I didn't realize the land is red."

"You don't hear it much now," the premier said, "but years ago islanders were called Redfeet, like Nova Scotians are called Bluenoses."

"The soil sure sticks," I said. "The farmers couldn't get it off their boots when they went in the hall."

"You can imagine what happens to farm machinery in that gumbo," Mr. Jones said. "And to our cars and trucks on a lot of our roads."

"I noticed you talked quite a lot tonight about asphalt," I said.

"No political meeting in Prince Edward Island can do without asphalt," he said, "whether it's lack of, according to the Conservatives, or ribbons of it, as we Liberals claim."

There was practically no traffic and we hummed along through the black November night. The secretary, about 50, I guessed, put her head against the premier's shoulder and went to sleep. He sang a little tune, and then whistled softly. I tried to talk island politics but he was tired of the subject. Yet he didn't mind talking about the land, or the potato crop, or the declining fox industry, or oyster farming. He named off every hamlet we ran through and told me what the crops had been like there during the war, and since, and the prices potatoes had fetched.

"I'm a green mountain man myself," I said, naming one of the two varieties of spuds I remembered (the other was purple cobbler) from my farm summers in New Brunswick.

"Are you now?" Mr. Jones said. "I prefer any round white, really." The green mountain is oblong. He discussed how different varieties fared in different soils and their fertilizer needs. I learned more about Prince Edward Island than I thought would have been possible.

He dropped me at the hotel and I went to my room to write a Tignish story. I filed it at the telegraph office a few blocks away and went to bed.

There was hell to pay in the morning. Old Mr. Burnett, the publisher of the *Guardian*, summoned me to his office. He got to the point fast.

"What right have you to come over here and hold islanders up to ridicule? I've reported you to Brayley." Jack Brayley was my Canadian Press boss in Halifax. Each newspaper in Canada owned a piece of CP.

I asked him what he meant.

"All that stuff about our farmers tramping into the meeting at Tignish with red mud on their boots as if they were country hicks with no manners."

"I was just trying to put in some local color," I explained.

"Don't be smart with me, young man. I won't have our people being made fun of across the country by some pup from the mainland."

He was really sore. I tried to tell him I'd been a farm boy myself, and why would I ridicule my own kind?

He would have none of it and dismissed me as a disgrace to the newspaper business. I went back to the hotel and poured myself a riveter from my prescription bottle.

There was worse to come.

Cal Lewis came to my room just before the big Conservative rally the next night.

"I hear you got it good from the old man," he said.

"He didn't beat around the bush," I said.

"He's not so bad," Cal said.

I invited Cal to have a drink before we went over to the meeting together.

"Maybe just a sip," he said. I poured him a tiny one and he downed it and I put some more rum in his glass. I shouldn't have. I didn't know Cal was an alcoholic (shako was the local word) who was trying heroically to stay on the wagon. He was accommodating me because of the run-in I'd had with his publisher, but the two drinks, plus a follow-up one, pushed him over the edge and he passed out cold on the bed.

I tried my best to rouse him, but couldn't, and left him there and went to the meeting. I came back and wrote my story and telephoned the telegraph office to have a messenger come over and pick it up.

Then I set to work to write Cal's story. This was not an unusual practice. At a Maritime convention of the United Mine Workers in Truro the year before, four of us had combined to cover for the reporter of the Sydney *Post-Record*, out of it with drink, for five days. But we'd had time to study his style and the newspaper's editorial quirks before we filed the copy. I had done no such research on Cal or the *Guardian*. But I wrote a piece and delivered it to the *Guardian* office, saying Cal had asked me to bring it in because he was working on another, related story. With the help of the night clerk, I then got Cal down the elevator and into a taxi home.

It didn't work. The copy desk at the *Guardian* twigged right away that Cal hadn't written it. And it was far too short an account of *the* Conservative meeting of the campaign. When the night editor went looking for Cal for more copy, my amateurish cover-up was exposed.

I found out all this when Brayley phoned me. I knew it was serious because Canadian Press hardly ever used the long-distance telephone.

"Don't go near the *Guardian*," Jack said. "Burnett has called Purcell in Toronto and says you deliberately got his man drunk so you could get a scoop on that meeting." Gillis Purcell was CP's general manager.

"But . . . " I said.

"Stay under cover and come right back after the election," Jack said. He hung up.

I reported the Liberal win (24 seats to 6) and returned to the hotel. Cal was waiting for me in the lobby.

"You been fired?" I asked anxiously.

"No," he said. "That was the question I wanted to ask you."

"Not yet, anyway," I said.

"I'm sorry I passed out in your room," Cal said. "I should have told you my problem."

"I'm sorry I hashed up that piece I wrote," I said. "If I'd taken more time we might have got away with it."

"Not a chance," Cal said. "The *Guardian* wanted the name of practically everyone there."

"I suppose old man Burnett gave it to you worse than he gave it to me," I said.

"He had words, all right," Cal said. "But he won't fire me. I'll tell you why."

Cal led the way over to a couple of lobby chairs and we sat down.

Cal said he'd done five years in Dorchester penitentiary for shooting and wounding a Mountie who'd surprised him bottling prime stuff from his still, hidden (he thought) in a wood on the western end of the island. Cal had simply whirled and fired his shotgun before identifying the target.

"When I got out, nobody'd give me a job. But Mr. Burnett did."

"I see," I said. I didn't.

"Exactly," Cal said. "Mr. Burnett has to believe in me, he wants to believe in me. Then I fall down drunk on him again. It's far easier for him to believe that you got me drunk than that I did it to myself."

"Let's finish the bottle," I said.

"Good night," he said.

I polished it off alone. When I headed for the Borden train the next morning, Mr. Foster was in the lobby.

"Come again real soon," he called out.

There was a telegram for me when I got back to Halifax. It was from Cal, and said, "All is serene. It was all your fault."

I wasn't fired, either.

Pulling
Nets

In May, 1948, I went to Newfoundland to report on the Confederation debates. I flew to St. John's in a Trans-Canada Air Lines DC-3 *Dakota*, and the gorgeous stewardess talked to me nearly all the way from Halifax because there were only three passengers, and the other two were old. I have flown Air Canada ever since, though the stewardesses, now flight attendants, no longer talk to me, but then they ignore all the other passengers, too.

Newfoundland had been run as a British colony since 1933, when it went broke in the Depression and had to give up self-government. The war had improved things a bit economically, and though most of them were still as poor as church mice, Newfoundlanders wanted their independence back, as a self-governing country in the Commonwealth or as a province of Canada. It took a constituent assembly and two referendums to settle the issue, and the outcome is generally known.

St. John's was the seat of the self-government crowd and pretty hostile to Canada. Visiting Canadians, like me, were apt to be regarded as secret agents of Ottawa, paid or unpaid.

"What are you doing here, bugger-lugs?" was the greeting of a man to whom I'd just been introduced in the capital's best-known drinking establishment, the Crow's Nest, from which the Canadian Navy was run during the war. The girl on the switchboard at the Newfoundland Hotel where I was staying regularly cut off my telephone calls with an explosive "Canadian spy!"

I made my daily rounds of the Confederates and the Self-Governors and talked to as many other people as I could for material for my stories. I covered the length of Water Street at least once a day. But even not counting the restraints of the switchboard, I felt isolated in the hotel. It didn't seem to be part of Newfoundland at all. The dining-room waiters wore tails, even at breakfast, and Newfoundland dishes never appeared on the menu. The place was an English seaside relic. For all the time I was there, a British Broadcasting Corporation crew lived in the hotel. The six of them, five men and a woman, spent hours in the dining room getting drunk and abusing their waiter, as only Englishmen can do. I could never find out what they were doing.

"A big documentary," one told me one day.

"What about?"

"All of Newfoundland," he said with an elaborate gesture taking in the whole island.

"You haven't been out of St. John's," I said. I hadn't been either, but that was different.

"Oh, that will come later when the weather gets warmer," the BBC man said.

"What have you found in St. John's so far?" I asked. I thought he might have an angle that I could steal.

"My dear chap, these things can't be rushed. We're still laying it all out."

One day, instead of walking west along Water Street from the hotel, which was at the east end of the city at the foot of Signal Hill, I walked in the opposite direction, down Battery Road. It was a narrow dirt lane skirting the base of Signal Hill along the north side of the Narrows, the entrance to the harbor. Perched over the Narrows were dozens of shacks, a few small houses, flakes (platforms on stilts for drying fish) and rough wharves for fishing boats. The community is called the Battery and is, in effect, a Newfoundland outport plunked down at the eastern extremity of the city. St. John's at the time was poor and shabby for the most part, but it was rich and beautifully dressed compared with the Battery.

There didn't seem to be anybody around except for a few children playing in the street, the only ground even partly level, and then I noticed that most of the wharves were boatless. I'd come back later in the day after my dutiful political rounds.

For my pains, I got another glowing report from Joey Smallwood on his Confederation campaign in the eastern outports ("very big in Fogo," he said, "very big") and another lecture from Peter Cashin on why Newfoundland should go back to the gold standard, which had been discarded by the world. But old Mr. Jeffery, the editor of the *Evening Telegram*, heartened me when I told him I'd gone down to the Battery. "Good," he said, "that's the real Newfoundland, at least in this part of the island."

When I returned to the Battery, the boats were back and fish were being thrown on the wharves and flakes. Some nets were being unravelled. Two men in rubber boots were standing outside an unpainted shack. On the spur of the moment, I said, "How about taking me out with you?"

They looked me over. "A little scrawny for the work," one said. Postwar, I'd fleshed out to 135 pounds.

I told him I was a reporter and wanted to know something about how Newfoundlanders lived. It sounded ludicrous.

"Hand to mouth," the older man said.

"Where are you staying?" the other asked. I told him, the Newfoundland Hotel.

"You sure won't find out there," he said.

I was going to say I already knew that, but suddenly remembered something and said, "Except for the liquor store." There was a small Dutch door near the reception desk where you could knock and be sold a bottle.

They grinned. "Okay," the older man said. "But come tonight because we'll be going out real early."

After dinner at the hotel (roast beef and Yorkshire) I knocked at the little Dutch door, bought four bottles of rum, wondering how I was going to get them on my expense account without challenge, put on my oldest (that is, everyday) clothes and picked my way to the shack in the Battery. It wasn't easy in the dark; there were no street lights.

There were four men in the tiny building. There were no chairs because it was too crowded for such furniture. There were double bunks on three sides of the shack; the door, a shelf and a food locker on the fourth side; and a round stove in the centre of the one room. There

was one window, over the shelf. Three men were sitting
on lower bunks and one was standing beside the narrow
shelf. There was no sink or toilet.

I introduced myself to Danny and John, whom I
judged to be in their forties, and to Art and Joe, who
were about my age (26). They were big men, except for
John, who was wiry. It was Danny and Art I'd met earlier. I put the rum down on the shelf and Danny produced five glasses that had seen a lot of wear and tear. I
poured a good dollop into each glass and looked around
for some water.

"Joe, go get a pail of water at the house," Danny said.
"And as long as you're at it, take those dishes." Joe went
out with the dirty dishes.

"They have to be washed at my house," Danny said.
"It's down the street a ways. While we're fishing we live
in the shack together as much as we can. It's a little
crowded, but it's handy. John, here, lives over town."

The three of them drank the rum straight, and so did
Joe when he came back with the water. I was the only
one who cut it. We sat on the bunks, our chins nearly
over the stove, which wasn't lit.

"You have to lie well back from the stove when she's
going," Joe said.

They made polite remarks about the rum and didn't
waste any time with it. We talked about the coming
vote for a while, but the subject didn't interest them all
that much.

"Nothing's going to change for us," Danny said. "It'll
still be cod, cod, cod."

"Maybe you'll get higher prices," I said.

"They've been saying that since I was a boy in Carbon-
ear," Danny said. "When the war came along, they asked

us to keep the prices down. The Bowrings did all right, though, like they always do." He was referring to the leading St. John's merchants, Newfoundland's chief symbol of wealth.

But none of them was whining about his lot. Far from it. They joked and bantered and asked what Joey Smallwood was telling me.

"I knew Joey when he didn't have a pot to piss in or a window to throw it out of," Danny said.

He was amused that Joey was now being called an apostle—of Confederation, or anything else.

"Will we get those baby bonuses like Joey says?" John asked.

"If you vote right," I said.

"Joey says we won't have to pay Customs duties any more on our mail orders from Simpson's and Eaton's," Art said.

"There's one thing Joey isn't telling you about," I said. "You don't have a sales tax, but Canada has."

Danny slapped his knee. "I knew it," he said delightedly. "I knew there'd be something Joey would be holding back."

They all laughed.

"That Joey," John said.

They kept to themselves how they were going to vote and I was wise enough not to ask them. I'd been told often enough in St. John's, "None of your damn business." Which, of course, it wasn't.

Almost before I knew it, two of the rum bottles were empty and we were working our way through the third. They still took the booze neat, and even though I was mixing in water liberally from the pail I could feel myself getting sloshed.

When I had to pee, Danny said, "Joe, show him where."

"I don't need any help for that," I said.

"It's a little tricky," Joe said.

The light from the one unshaded bulb hanging from the ceiling of the shack shone dimly through the dirty window to a rocky path.

"This way," Joe said. "Watch out, it's some steep."

The path itself wasn't steep, but the rockwall on one side fell a straight 10 feet to a flake. We reached the communal privy at the end of the 50-yard track and made it back again, but I vowed I'd wait for daylight before I ventured out there again.

I didn't remember a great deal after that. I came to on a lower bunk with heat on my face. The stove was going and from a top bunk Danny was flopping bacon. He could easily reach the frying pan on the top of the stove while propped up on one elbow, fork in free hand.

Breakfast was bacon, bread and, in my case, water from the pail. I had a terrible thirst.

"No time for coffee today," Danny said.

There was the faintest trace of dawn when we made our way down to the two boats, Danny, Art and I in one and John and Joe in the other. Art cranked the engine; it caught on the second try and we chugged out through the Narrows, John trailing.

I appreciated the cool breeze on my fevered face but the sea became choppy outside the harbormouth and put the whitecap on my hangover. It wasn't the worst hangover I've ever had, but it was right up there. The worst was to come 12 years later in Freetown, Sierra Leone. I was being driven through town on a bright morning, eyes closed, head in hand, praying for survival. Suddenly I opened my eyes and found myself staring into the hideous face of a bald-headed, red-beaked (from blood) vulture. I screamed. The driver gently explained that the vultures were protected as street-cleaning garbage disposals.

"Where are we going?" I shouted at Danny.

"Just a few miles out where our nets are set," he shouted back.

I thought I knew something about dead weights from pushing rocks onto the stone-boat and lifting barrels of potatoes on my uncle's farm. But nothing could ever be heavier than those fishing nets, with or without cod in them. I strained every muscle trying to bring the nets alongside and far enough into the boat to retrieve the fish. Danny or Art had to help me every time, and I ended up just being in the way.

But I was determined that no Newfoundlander was going to put down a mainlander and I kept at it. My breaking back made a good companion for my aching head. After an hour, my hands were sore, even under the thick mitts Danny had given me. Danny and Art whistled or hummed while they worked, pausing only to give me an encouraging wink.

Somehow I lived through the next two hours. I was so tired I couldn't even remember I had a hangover. When the nets had been reset and we'd started back, Danny said, "You look as if you could stand a drink."

My rum was all gone, of course, but Danny sent Art for some. I said I'd go back to the hotel for a new supply, but they wouldn't allow it.

"You brought your share," Danny said. "You'd never make it anyway. And if you did, you'd never make it back."

I practically crawled up over the flakes to the shack and flopped on a lower bunk. I pained all over. I shut my eyes and prayed for enough strength to walk back to the hotel after a while.

Danny pulled me up to a sitting position and handed me an unwashed glass.

"Better try this one straight," he said.

It was powerful and I nearly choked.

"What's this?" I asked.

"Swish," Danny said. "The very best."

"Swish?"

"We buy empty rum barrels from the liquor commission, pour boiling water in the bottom, swish it around, and we get the rum that's soaked into the wood. We can get a gallon easy from a barrel we pay a dollar for."

"No wonder that tame stuff I brought went so fast," I said.

"No need to apologize," Danny said. "It's not your fault the liquor commission cuts the rum by a good half."

The swish improved my condition considerably and I asked for another—with water. Danny left me on the bunk and joined the others to unload the boat, open the fish, spread them on the flakes and salt them down. When I woke from a doze, the men were sitting on the other two bunks with their drinks. John put some bacon on the stove.

"I'll fry up some potatoes, too," he said, rummaging in the food locker under the window.

"How do you like the fisherman's life?" Joe asked, looking around the shack.

"Great," I said, lying through the swish.

"Maybe you'd like to go out again tomorrow," Danny said. "We figure on moving a few nets some south towards Bay Bulls."

"Sure," I said. Too much swish already, but I had to show these Newfoundlanders I could hack more than one measly day.

We had bacon and fried potatoes and swish, and before long I was out like a light, while they talked on, apparently as fresh as daisies. They had more stamina than Clydesdales.

In the morning, I went down to the wharf on only slightly less rubbery legs. John was starting his boat in the squat wheelhouse. Without warning, the crank kicked back and his left arm snapped.

"Damn," he said, as if it had been a scratch. Danny looked over from his boat.

"She's broke," John said, holding up his arm to show the bend between the wrist and the elbow.

"That's tough," Danny said.

"Where do we phone for a doctor?" I asked.

"We don't have a phone," Danny said.

"I'll run and call from the hotel," I said.

"No," Danny said. "No doctor would come down here anyway."

"I'll go get a taxi," I said.

"John will look after himself," Danny said.

John was already walking up to the road, his right hand clamped over the break to keep the two ends of bone from rubbing each other.

"I'll go with you," I called.

"I know the way," John said sharply and kept on going.

"Why won't he let us do anything?" I asked.

"He's mad at himself for such a stupid accident," Danny said. "And he's mad because there won't be any money till the arm heals. He's just mad."

"What about workmen's compensation?" I asked.

"No such thing here," Danny said. "Or unemployment insurance. And we can't afford our own insurance. It'll be bad enough for John to have to pay the hospital for setting his arm. That'll be hanging over him till he can start working again."

I said I still didn't understand why John wouldn't let me go with him.

"It's not you," Danny said. "He wouldn't want any of us to go, either. He knows we have to get out to the nets. And you'd embarrass him by getting a taxi and paying for it. He'll walk. It's only a mile or so."

I went in Danny's boat again and Art joined Joe in John's. I tried twice as hard at the nets but I wasn't much help.

"Another week and you'd get the hang of it," Danny said. There was some respite this time with the resetting of some nets about six miles to the south.

When we got back, John was sitting on the wharf with his arm in a cast. He hadn't even gone home after the hospital.

"Taking it easy already," Danny said to him.

"I can still mend a net," John said.

"One for the road," I said, when we were in the shack again. I downed it, unmixed, in a quick gulp.

"Come again," Danny said.

"Thanks for the fishing lesson," I said.

"I don't think Newfoundland is quite ready for you," Danny said.

The four of them walked me up the road as far as the bend where the hotel came into view. We shook hands gravely and I walked the rest of the way alone. I felt a twinge of guilt when I crawled into the soft hotel bed. But it didn't keep me from sleeping 12 hours straight.

Talking to Bud

You know the great Canadian mystique: how drab and divided we all were until four decades ago when a national spirit of animated oneness was born out of a single football game, the 1948 Grey Cup?

More than most myths, it has been a huge success, generating true patriot love and, much more important to Canadians, economic benefits. From a Saturday afternoon sporting event, it grew into a week-long extravaganza with bulging planeloads of fans (ungraciously described by airline pilots as "animal flights"), stuffed hotels, parades outdoing Santa Claus's, cash flow, and the mandatory downtown street riot, sometimes with looting.

I bet you can't name the principals in that myth-making championship game on November 27, 1948, or the winner, or the score. All you probably remember, or have learned since, is what you've been spoon-fed: a Toronto pop-eyed at a Calgary Stampede reincarnated amid the bank towers; and beautifully caparisoned white stallions ridden by 10-gallon-hatted, chapped and

spurred cowboys—right into the heart of the Commonwealth, the lobby of the Royal York Hotel.

Chuckwagons are said to have thundered to City Hall,
where flapjacks cooked on their tailboards were gobbled
down by eastern masses agog at western hospitality and
vitality. Toronto the good and introverted had been mag-
ically transformed into Toronto the naughty and extro-
verted. This good cheer, the myth continues, radiated
east and west at the speed of sound, and Canada suddenly became one big, happy family, regional differences
put aside forever.

It's all buffalo chips.

I was there and helped spread some of those chips
myself.

Ordinarily, I'm no debunker, and the myth surrounding the Grey Cup of 1948 has more substance than others we've heard: John Diefenbaker's northern vision,
Pierre Trudeau's wrestling of inflation to the ground,
and Brian Mulroney's rejection of patronage. But I think
it's time to come clean.

I was a Canadian Press reporter in the Toronto office
—on refreshment from the Halifax bureau—on Friday,
November 26, 1948, the day before the game. I had no
assignment connected with it. But I was seen to be
momentarily idle, and the nearest deskman dispatched
me to Union Station to meet the morning train bearing
the Calgary Stampeder fans. No provision had been
made beforehand to cover such a triviality.

The fans who tumbled off that train looked little different from anybody else who has ridden a transconti-
nental for three days. The few women looked fine, but
the men were unshaven and most of them had a hangover or a jag on. The first fan I interviewed did not say

"Yippee!" or "Yea, Stamps." He said, "Where can I get a drink?" These were no ordinary fans; they could afford the expensive fancy clothes and to take at least a week off work. That's why there were so few of them—and no cowboys at all.

Did I report this in my story carried across Canada? Not on your life. I was playing an unknown hand in creating the myth that a football game led to the rebirth (or birth) of national conciliation.

There were only 180 fans on the 17-car "special" (CP reported on the Monday after the game that 500 fans were returning to Calgary by train), one Sarcee Indian chief, seven horses and one small chuckwagon. Out of this meagre assembly all the reporters at the station, including me, made out that a Calgary Stampede bigger than the original had roared into downtown Toronto.

Let me go back to the start of that week. The Stampeders, the western champions by virtue of their best-of-three-games victory over Edmonton, sneaked into—there is no other description—Toronto at 7 a.m., Sunday, November 21, and were met at the station by a porter. No wonder. They hadn't won a national title since 1911.

The arrival barely made the Monday sports pages. The president of the team, Tom Brooks, coach Les Lear and quarterback Keith Spaith didn't even accompany the team. They flew from Calgary to Ottawa to scout the eastern final, which the Ottawa Rough Riders won by beating Hamilton 19-0. The Stamps practised in complete obscurity all week at Appleby College in Oakville and put up at a highway dine-and-dance joint called the Pig 'n' Whistle, also in Oakville. For off-field recreation, they took in a hockey game at Maple Leaf Gardens and went to see Niagara Falls. Wow.

The Calgary team had arrived one day after *the* parade in Toronto—the annual Santa Claus ride—and the Grey Cup was ignored by the front pages of the Toronto newspapers nearly all week. An airport picture of Brooks, Lear and Spaith, taken during their plane-change in Toronto, made page 24 of the *Telegram*. Pre-game *Telegram* stories made page 22 on the Tuesday and page 24 on the Wednesday.

On the Thursday and Friday before the Saturday game, the headline in both the *Telegram* and *Globe and Mail* was the sale of the *Telegram* to *Globe* publisher George McCullagh for $3.61 million. There's nothing like a story about Toronto newspapers to excite Toronto newspapers. The *Tely's* Thursday reference to the Grey Cup game was on page 26. On the same day *Globe* sports columnist Jim Coleman wrote about hockey.

On the day before the game, the big story in both *Telegram* and *Star* was "2 Quarrel, Brother Shot" (*Telegram*); "Brother Held After Man Shot" (*Star*). But there was a front-page story in the *Star* under the head "Union Station Stampeded As Calgarians Roar In." It more than doubled to 400 the number of Calgary fans on the train. The Calgary *Herald* headlined the fans' arrival with: "Stampeder Fans Put On Western Show For East."

The show was a square dance in Union Station, by the few still capable, before an audience of about a hundred, mostly passengers from other trains and station employees. The Calgarians then trailed across Front Street to the Royal York, and the *Herald* gushed that "traffic was held up for ten minutes." Wow.

The Rough Riders also arrived by train that day and were almost universally ignored.

On Saturday, there was a fair-sized crowd (because people worked Saturdays then) at City Hall around the single chuckwagon where some flapjacks were cooked but mostly (and wisely) uneaten. In Calgary, workers bought small radios so they could listen to the broadcast of the game at the office or factory.

Toronto Mayor Hiram McCallum wore a 10-gallon (actually, two-quart) hat and rode a horse. Nothing as indecorous had ever been seen in Toronto outside Shea's vaudeville house. The rag-tag parade from City Hall to Varsity Stadium comprised the little chuckwagon and eight or nine horses. There was practically nothing in the papers about the parade because the press devoted all its space to accounts of the game itself. In those days, newspapers published late editions, even on Saturday, so that they could actually print the news on the day it happened.

The weather was good for November, but there wasn't a record crowd. Ticket prices were $1 and $1.50, and the gate receipts amounted to $26,655 from a crowd of 20,013. The record at Varsity Stadium was 20,680—for a college game.

The game at the time became known for two plays: the last Grey Cup sleeper play, and a bonehead Ottawa error that allowed Calgary's winning touchdown. On the sleeper, Calgary end Norm Hill ran to the sidelines and flopped down on the grass. Everybody saw him except the Ottawa players on the field. Quarterback Spaith threw to the uncovered Hill for a touchdown. Ottawa blew the game when it neglected to fall on a loose ball fumbled by Pete Karpuk on a lateral pass. The Riders stood and gawked while Calgary's Woody Strode picked it up and ran, lateralled to Jim Mitchener, who reached the Ottawa 10-yard line, from where Pete Thodos scored on the next play. The Stamps won 12-7.

The Saturday night celebration was hardly raucous. There was some square-dancing in the Royal York lobby, but without any horse—white stallion or whatever. Three musicians did stand on a table. A hotel executive made a remark that would be considered insulting today: "No, we don't budget for extra breakage during the season, or for the Dominion final." (The word Dominion was still acceptable then.)

In Calgary, the beer parlor waiters complained that they had been unable to listen to the game on radio because the Alberta Liquor Control Act made it illegal to provide entertainment of any sort in licensed beverage rooms. Not even small radios were permitted in the tap-rooms out back. There was a bit of a snake dance in downtown Calgary (no arrests) but a civic holiday could not be held until the following Wednesday, when the train got in with team and fans.

Premier E.C. Manning of Alberta issued this statement: "My congratulations to Calgary and her splendid football team. The players and the supporters have brought credit not only to Calgary but to the whole province by their victory and their display of real western spirit." Wow.

Nothing from Manning about national unity breaking out, a subject which drew no editorial attention from newspapers. The Calgary *Herald* on Monday, November 29, carried an editorial—the editorial page cartoon that day was about Palestine—saying that "the old western spirit isn't dead, not by a jugful." Jugful was the operative word.

But hockey was still the real game. It didn't even have to be the Stanley Cup; the so-called amateur champi-

onship of Canada would do. The *Herald* editorial concluded: the Stampeders "will leave a bright mark on the
Canadian sports record. And now for the Allan Cup."

I must confess that my role in the Grey Cup myth is
very modest. The real myth-maker was Dorothy
Howarth of the *Telegram*, who wrote after the game:

> What statesmen at Royal Commissions and interna-
> tional conferences have failed to do since the days of
> Confederation, two handfuls of honest, hard-hitting
> top-grade athletes did all in the short space of three
> hours. They united Eastern and Western Canada into
> a strong bond of understanding and good-fellowship.

I went back to the Canadian Press office after the Grey
Cup parade left City Hall for Varsity Stadium, wrote a
parade story and was disconsolately looking out the
window into University Avenue when Ernie Burritt, the
news editor, said to me, "Let's go."

"Go where?" I said.

"To the game, of course."

I thought he was kidding.

"All you have to do is carry this bag," Ernie said.

It was a doctor's medical bag, and heavy. I thought
Ernie must be some kind of volunteer for the St. John
Ambulance Brigade.

I toted the bag, we got a cab and easily found our way
to good seats in the west-side covered stand. When we
were comfortable, Ernie said, "Get out the medicine."

"I'm okay," I said.

"Well, I'm not," he said.

I opened the bag and took out the bottle of rum,
glasses and mix. There was another bottle in reserve.

"Dammit, you forgot the ice," Ernie said.

In November, 1957, I was pitchforked into Grey Cup coverage again. This time I was standing around the Toronto Canadian Press office late on Friday before next day's game when it was discovered that no one had been sent to Varsity Stadium to report on Winnipeg Blue Bombers' final practice. "Oh, my God," everybody shouted, and all eyes peered around accusingly and then fell on me simultaneously. Away I went.

It was dark when I reached the stadium, and the Bombers were just coming off the field. The darkness didn't matter because I didn't know any of their faces. What to do? What to do?

My beat was national defence, external affairs and politics, but I did know the name of the Winnipeg coach, Bud Grant, and I had once (in 1939) seen the legendary Fritz (Twinkletoes) Hansen play for the Bombers. What better credentials could there be?

By this time, it was so dark that flashlights appeared on the field to guide the last stragglers to the dressing room under the west stand. I groped around. "Mr. Grant? Mr. Grant?"

"Back there," everybody said.

The last figure I could make out passed near me and I hailed it through the gloom. "Mr. Grant?"

"Yes," the figure said. "Can I help you?"

"You sure can," I said.

"What would you like to know?"

I quickly figured out there was no way I could fool him that I knew anything about football. So I blurted it all out: the regular guy had gone missing and I was the unknowledgeable replacement.

"Well, let's see what we can do," Grant said. "Ready?" He stood in the murk, making no move to go, while I hauled out my notebook and pencil. I couldn't see the book but I scribbled away as he talked. He covered everything, including answers to questions I'd never have thought of. We stood out on the cold field for nearly 15 minutes. I still think Bud Grant is the greatest man I ever met.

The other reporters were in the dressing room and Grant went over the same ground with them, but not in the same detail. I was able to make out most of my notes when I got back to the office.

"I didn't realize you knew football so well," said Fos Barclay, the deskman.

"It's a sideline," I said nonchalantly.

Hamilton Tiger-Cats beat the Blue Bombers 32-7. Grant hadn't mentioned to me, let alone complain, that his team had been badly hurt in the three-game western final with Edmonton. The last game had gone to two overtime periods.

Ernie wasn't there to take me to that game. He had died in 1951 at age 45.

Observation Car

The small ferry—she wasn't much bigger than a tug-boat—beat through a choppy First Narrows under Lions Gate Bridge and out into rougher water beyond. We pitched and rolled and the rain came down in buckets, drumming against the window of the tiny passenger cabin. We couldn't see one hundred yards ahead, let alone the mountains which, we were assured, rose spectacularly to our starboard. What a way to begin a vacation.

We yawed around Horseshoe Bay and up Howe Sound and in two hours or so reached Squamish, the then tidewater railhead of the Pacific Great Eastern Railway. My wife and I were bound for the interior ghost town of Barkerville at the end of the Cariboo Road. We had been transferred from Halifax to Vancouver in 1950 and wanted to see as much of British Columbia as possible before the next shift, probably to dreaded central Canada. We'd already done the Okanagan, Thompson and Fraser Valleys and southern Vancouver Island. I'd been to the Queen Charlotte Islands.

Jean wished to avoid (and so did I, to tell the truth) another trip through the Fraser Canyon. We'd made two by car, but our first trip, by train in 1950, had been the really unnerving one. We had wakened in the morning at Lytton, where the dusty Thompson meets the glacial Fraser. Jean pulled open the window curtains and was looking into space. The train, or at least our car, was parked on the high bridge and we were peering straight down into boiling water. The Pacific Great Eastern, for part of its journey to its northern terminus at Quesnel, ran along the banks of the Fraser, but it did not venture through the canyon.

The PGE was said by British Columbians, except those in Squamish and Quesnel, to go from nowhere to nowhere. It was the butt of bad jokes: Please Go Easy, Province's Greatest Expense, that kind of thing.

The PGE was started in 1912 to connect Vancouver with Prince George and the Grand Trunk Pacific. By 1915, 120 miles of steel had been put down to Lillooet. The next year, the contractors went broke—the fashion then for railroad builders—and the British Columbia government took it over to protect its heavy subsidy. Steel reached Lone Butte in 1919, Williams Lake in 1920, and in October, 1921, the first train ran 467 miles from Squamish to Quesnel. Some track was laid north of Quesnel but in 1942 it was ripped up for war scrap. Prince George was finally reached in late 1952 but the gap between Squamish and North Vancouver wasn't closed until 1956. The PGE made it to Dawson Creek in 1958, 13 years after the government had announced the northern extension.

The train standing in the station at Squamish was older than most trains of its day. It comprised a steam engine, coal tender, two freight cars, a baggage car, a coach, a diner-sleeper, an empty flatcar, which I presumed was for lumber to be loaded en route, and a caboose. The passengers were a mixed bag of miners, woodsmen and farmers, Indian and white. It was pretty late in the season and Jean and I seemed to be the only tourists.

We had a small compartment at one end of the diner. The dining section was a long wooden counter that looked like a bar in a frontier saloon (and probably had been) with stools instead of a footrail. There was one other compartment and two sections of bunks, upper and lower. We were the only occupants of the car. It was not your CNR or CPR parlor car, dining car or sleeper. But it was as clean as a new willow whistle.

After a delay that nobody, especially the train crew, seemed to notice, or care about, we panted away uphill to Brackendale, Garibaldi, Alta Lake, Pemberton, Creekside, Birken and D'Arcy. The train never travelled at a greater speed than 25 m.p.h., even when it reached the upland meadows, and it stopped much more often than at the stations I have listed. Like a streetcar, it halted wherever anybody asked to be let off, or waved to be let on. In any case, the crew seemed to know everybody's stop—usually, a footpath leading off into the dripping woods or across a small pasture to a log cabin and a small log barn. Only once was a passenger met: three running children rushed into the embrace of an Indian woman, laden with a large and full satchel, as she took the last high step off the coach to the cinders. By the time we reached Pemberton, the rain had stopped and the heavy cloud was dissipating quickly. We'd covered about 50 miles in four hours.

In the dining end of our car, the tall stools were empty and there was only a sinewy little man behind the counter. He wore a chef's cap, a clean apron and tattoos on his bare forearms, which were folded on his side of the wide counter.

We sat down opposite him. "Do you have a menu, please?" I asked.

"It's right here," he said, pointing to his head.

"Okay, let's hear it," I said.

"Boiled potatoes," he said.

"Have you any baked?" Jean asked.

"No," he said, "just boiled."

"Anything else?" I asked.

"Sure. Carrots."

"Any other vegetable?"

"No, just carrots."

"Any fish?"

"No."

"How about meat?"

"Bacon," he said.

"That's it?"

"Yep. You can have bacon in the morning, too, if you're staying on."

"Wouldn't miss it," I said, and he frowned.

"I suppose you're wondering about the menu," he said.

I allowed that the question had occurred to me.

"Well, we can't stock a whole lot of food when hardly anybody ever eats in here. All those people in the coach bring their own or wait till they get home."

"Somebody must go as far as Williams Lake or Quesnel," I said.

"Sure, that's why we have the diner. But it's mostly for the crew."

"Do they ever complain about the menu?" Jean asked.

"Every trip," he said.

"Have you been cook here long?" I asked.

"Chef," he said. "Since the war. I worked in the galley on corvettes during the war and before that I cooked in lumber and mining camps."

"Serve a lot of bacon?" I asked.

"It's a specialty of mine."

There was a long pause and he looked at us inquiringly.

"Well, what'll it be?" he said.

"I was thinking of bacon, boiled potatoes and carrots," Jean said.

"You hit it first crack," he said and turned to the stove.

"Do we have to wait for the potatoes to boil?" I asked.

"They're in the warming oven," he said. "And the carrots." He put bacon in the frying pan.

"Can you make it crisp?" I asked.

"I can, but it'll be black. Best take it as I do it."

It was warm, at least. The potato was the biggest I'd ever seen. He restored his elbows to the counter and watched us eat.

"Great potato," I said.

"They really grow out here on the coast," he said.

"Do you ever bake or roast or fry them?" Jean asked.

"Just boiled," he said.

"Do you have any coffee, please?" Jean asked.

"Tea."

"I think we'll both have tea," I said.

"Right."

After two cups of tea, I asked him what I owed him.

"Now, let's see, what did you have?" he said. I stared. He didn't bat an eye.

"Oh, yes, the bacon special," he said. "I guess that'll be a dollar each."

I gave him two dollars and a quarter.

"Have you tried the observation car?" he asked.

"Ha, ha," I said.

"I'm not kidding," he said. "That flatcar behind this one is the observation car. See for yourself. It's stopped raining so you won't get wet. Take this rag to wipe off one of the benches."

He was right. I hadn't noticed that some wooden benches were nailed to the flatcar. There were no railings, but the train travelled so slowly they didn't appear necessary. We walked halfway down the flatcar and selected a bench, which I wiped off with the rag he'd given me.

We sat down and looked around. It was magnificent. The sun was setting behind the Cayoosh Range off to our right, and the train, just away from its last stop at D'Arcy, was puffing along beside Anderson Lake. The dark was gathering in the lake valley while the sun was still glinting off the tops of the Shulaps Range ahead of us.

"Without dirty windows, you can see in every direction," I said needlessly. We turned around and sat looking back for a while. A man in the caboose waved to us. Oddly, there wasn't a trace of soot from the engine.

We just sat and looked and looked, switching our position now and then to concentrate on a different quarter of the compass. After a while, it started to get chilly.

"I'll get our sweaters," I said.

The chef was still standing behind the empty counter. I handed the rag back to him.

"Thanks for the tip about the flatcar," I said.

"Observation car," he said.

"It's different," I said.

"On a nice day, the coach passengers like to sit there. And the tourists like it, too, when we get any. Some of them complain about no handrails but we haven't lost anybody yet."

I fetched the sweaters and our bottle of rum. I asked the chef whether he could spare a couple of glasses.

"No, but here are two teacups. And take this flashlight, just in case a bear tries to climb aboard with you."

I looked hard at him. He didn't move a muscle.

"Have one yourself," I said, proffering him the bottle.

"Don't mind if I do, especially after a hard day like this one," he said. He nearly filled a teacup.

I returned to the observation car. Jean and I put on our sweaters and I poured a couple of straight rums into the chipped cups. We sipped and sipped and pretty soon the moon came up over Seton Lake, the one right after Anderson Lake. The rum took away the chill. We didn't say much but just kept looking at the moonlight on the lake and the enveloping mountains. Could anything anywhere be more beautiful? Only Cape Breton, we decided, specifically the Mabou Highlands. But that was Jean's loyalty to Cape Breton, and mine to her.

While we slept, the train reached Lillooet, skirted the Camelsfoot Range and continued north through Pavilion, Chasm, 70-Mile House and 100-Mile House to Williams Lake, where the line settled in on the east bank of the Fraser.

We woke up about Soda Creek, and our personal chef soon had the promised bacon on. We declined the potatoes and carrots in favor of toast. We rode the observation car while we drank our tea. The chef came out with the granite pot and refilled our cups.

We dismounted at Quesnel, the end of the line, and found the old hotel handy to the station. We left our one suitcase in the room and hunted up a taxi to take us to Barkerville, 60 gravelled miles to the east, and back. We agreed on 25 dollars, plus the cabbie's lunch at Wells on Jack of Clubs Lake.

When the gold rush swept into British Columbia in 1858, the miners took the trail north up the Fraser River. So did their camp-followers: storekeepers, cooks, bartenders, dancehall girls, blacksmiths, preachers, barbers, money lenders, bakers, prize fighters, bootleggers, liverymen, butchers, card sharps, quacks, newspapermen, shysters and gravediggers. All these good-time-Charlies quickly discarded each shacktown as its strike petered out and moved on behind the pan-shuttlers to the next golden creek. The Cariboo Road was built to supply them, and it is still the great north highway.

At Quesnel, the search for fortunes turned abruptly east, and the biggest strike of all was made on Williams Creek (the Klondike of its day) in 1861. Billy Barker sank his fabulous pit and Barkerville grew up around the hole until it had ten thousand people. Here the Cariboo Road ended in a dog-legged main drag only 18 feet wide which ran parallel to Williams Creek. There was an uneven boardwalk on each side. In 1862, 727 claims were staked; in 1863, 3,071. Billy Barker took out $600,000, married a London widow in Victoria and was broke by 1868, when the widow left him.

Barkerville burned down September 16, 1868, when, the story goes, a drunken miner was kissing a hurdy-gurdy girl in Alder's saloon, fell against the stove and dislodged the hot stovepipe going through the canvas roof. One hundred and sixteen houses were destroyed. The town was rebuilt, but gradually it disintegrated, without benefit of fire, as the $40 million seam of gold was exhausted.

There are said to be 788 curves on the Quesnel-Barkerville road. We didn't count, but there wasn't a straight stretch longer than 20 yards. We stirred up an additional layer of dust, like a battleship making camouflage smoke, to be deposited on the litter of nearly one hundred years. All along the sides of the road through Cottonwood, Wingdam and Stanley, each a ghost town, were crumbling shacks and sluice boxes, rusted iron, unexplainable machinery with trees piercing it, and hundreds of heaps of gravel sifted from creek beds. Traces of eight other gold towns along the road have vanished in the forest.

A few people still lived in Barkerville. (There are more now because the road is paved and there is an historic park, campground, ski area and two airfields in the vicinity, and all the attendant latter-day camp-followers.) We didn't see any of them. Most of the buildings had been beaten naked by the weather. Some had collapsed in on themselves; others had fallen over sideways. Through the shattered windows of the Nicol Hotel we could see dust-laden glasses still perched on shelves behind the curving bar. Mooseheads, antlers and bearskins adorned the cobwebbed walls.

Near the western end of the street stands St. Savior's tiny, wooden Anglican church, built in 1869. The vestry was papered with ads clipped from long-defunct magazines and contained an ancient vacuum cleaner, operated by a hand pump. There was only one plaque in the church, whose plank floor was scrubbed as clean as a small boy ready for Sunday school. The plaque remembers a trapper drowned long ago, and says:

He bade no one a last farewell,
He said good-bye to none;
The heavenly gates were opened wide,
A loving voice said, 'Come.'

Next door to the Nicol was a tavern in use, but with current British Columbia regulations: beer only; open 4 to
6, 7 to 11 p.m. The graveyard overlooks the town and
rushing Williams Creek. Weather had washed the names
from most of the wooden slabs marking the graves of
men who had come from all over North America and
Europe. There are no Chinese graves; "Celestials," as
they were called, were barred. Typhus was prevalent and
mine accidents, especially cave-ins, were common. The
cemetery is a young man's graveyard; only the young
and healthy could get this far.

Jean and I walked to the far end of the dog-eared
street. Beyond was wilderness. Straight east, over the
mountains: Yellowhead Pass and Jasper.

Herb the driver and Jean and I had a sandwich at
Wells in a new, rough-hewn restaurant.

"Why would you two come all the way out here on this
god-awful road to see those old buildings?" Herb asked.

"Same reason we went to San Francisco last year," I
said. "To see a town built on gold."

"I hear San Francisco lasted longer," he said.

We drove back to Quesnel. The dust hadn't entirely
settled from our trip in. I handed Herb 30 dollars and he
handed back the five-dollar tip.

"You've given me something to talk about," he said. "I
hadn't been out there for years, since I was a kid, I guess."

That evening Jean and I went down to the rowdy
hotel beer parlor.

The waiter said, "I'd advise you to take that table in the corner. It gets pretty rough in here Saturday nights."

He brought our draft beers. "Look," he said, "maybe I can build a little protection around you." Jean began to look slightly alarmed. The waiter moved two other tables so that we were hemmed into the corner behind solid furniture.

"That should do it, but keep your eyes peeled," he said.

"For what?" I said.

"Flying glass and bodies," he said.

"These guys are trying to relive Billy Barker days," I told Jean. "You'd think this was the Nicol Hotel."

We plugged away steadily at the beer. It got noisier and noisier. But apart from a little pushing and shoving and appropriate curses, nothing happened. We stayed till closing. We figured we might as well: our room was immediately above.

"Thanks for the barricade," I said to the waiter.

"Boy, she was real quiet tonight for a change," he said.

"Yeah," I said, with a cowboy drawl.

When we caught the Pacific Great Eastern back to Squamish, the observation car was missing. On the station platform I asked the conductor about it.

"We figured it was costing us too much to haul all the way up here for just two passengers," he said. "She's on the siding over there until next summer."

The
Second
Expulsion

I arrived in Jerusalem, New Brunswick, in an army jeep one warm summer day in 1955.

The driver stopped in front of the general store at the gravel intersection where the road ran off at right angles to West Jerusalem. We looked around. Nothing moved except the heat shimmer. The silence was complete. All the houses and barns and outbuildings were deserted, of people, animals, furnishings, machinery, goods—everything except broken and rusted scraps not worth carrying away.

We were in the middle of one of the oldest settled parts of New Brunswick, a 375-square-mile tract on the west bank of the St. John River expropriated three years before by the defence department as an exercise field for the Canadian Army. Eleven hundred families had been uprooted. Nothing had been left to the former occupants except their graveyards, which were the only pieces of ground off limits to the military. All the buildings were open to any army use—artillery shelling, infantry assault, bulldozing by tanks, incineration by flame-throwers: whatever fitted mock war.

I got out of the jeep and walked about a hundred yards up a dirt laneway overgrown with weeds to the nearest farmhouse. The windows were still intact. The back door was unlocked—it didn't appear that there had ever been a lock for it—and I stepped into the summer kitchen. A verse from a long piece of doggerel I had once read sprang to mind. How did it go?

> Alone, at the foot of the hill,
> Stands a grey and sad little house;
> It's been abandoned forever,
> Except by the spider and mouse.

The summer kitchen held only a broken wooden washing machine lying on its side, with one foot snapped off and the handle missing from the wringer. The sink was still in place, and beside it the shelf bearing two rings worn into the wood to show where thousands of pailfuls of water fetched from the well had been set down by weary arms. Dust that had blown in under the door covered the wide-plank floor.

The winter kitchen was even barer. The wood stove had been removed, with stovepipes. Doors had been stripped from cupboards, and the flour barrel and its iron swinging trestle were gone. The empty screw holes showed where the tall, wooden telephone had been clamped to the wall. All the other curtainless rooms were bare. Even the linoleum had been taken.

I knew country like this. I had spent nearly all my summers as a boy on my uncle's farm at Jacksontown in the St. John River Valley, 140 miles north of here. It had been abandoned a few years before, when there was no one left to work it. My sister and I went to Jacksontown for our Aunt Georgie's funeral. After she had been put in the ground, lovingly and tenderly, across the dusty road from the white church, we drove out to see the old place under the hill. It was a mistake. The barns had been pulled down for their timber and enormous weeds were choking the farmhouse to death. The happy kitchen, where as many as 14 of us used to gather for dinner at noon, was being rapidly destroyed by weather and porcupines. It was hard to believe that such a sturdy house could come apart so fast with nobody in it or to look after it. Later, the remains of the house and all the other buildings were ploughed under so that no one could even guess that four generations of the Mallory family had lived there. There was not even a hump or depression in the ground to show that the homestead had ever been anything except part of the field it was in.

I was now looking at the same thing, except that in the army's Camp Gagetown, abandonment—forced abandonment—was repeated eleven hundred times.

The expropriation of 282,000 acres was carried out by the defence department in 1952 without a word of consultation with the residents. They found out from an Ottawa press release in the newspapers that their land, first settled by their forbears in 1783, was being taken away from them, without appeal. Nobody had asked them. No member of the government had come down from Ottawa to talk it over. Even when the surveyors began measuring the land, like uncaring tailors for unknown customers, no official appeared to discuss what was happening. Only after the announcement of the expropriation on August 1, 1952, by Defence Minister Brooke Claxton, did the government instal an office to work out the compensation for each family. The office was established in Fredericton, 60 miles away. An office in Jerusalem was out of the question: apart from electricity, which it got in 1948, the village didn't have the amenities expected and demanded by civil servants. The residents were given one year to clear out.

There were other acreages in New Brunswick that the defence department could have bought without putting anybody off the land. But it explained that they were forested, and it was cheaper to expropriate farmland than to pay for woods-clearing. The entire project cost $30 million, and that included all the camp construction to accommodate twenty-thousand troops on exercise and a large permanent staff. The average payment for a farm of some 200 acres was about $3,000. Most of the farmers moved to neighboring Kings County.

I left the house and its shrunken, untended dahlias and went out past the wellhouse to the barns. Some swallows were dive-bombing in the cow barn where the wooden stanchions stood forlornly empty. There was no manure pile. Had the occupant spread it on his fields in a last defiant gesture of proper and tidy farming methods? Most of the farms in the district made and sold butter from the milk of their Holstein, Ayrshire and Jersey herds. In 1938, the creamery at Harvey had begun picking up cream in the area.

The floor of the horsebarn was worn deep by a hundred years of iron shoes, and the cobwebs on the windows had all but shut out the daylight. There was a broken horserake in the machine shed and a torn canvas from a Frost and Wood binder. The chicken wire, mended and re-mended, had been left around the henhouse.

I walked back to the jeep. There was another jeep parked beside it with a soldier-driver and a civilian.

"I see that you're examining the second expulsion of the Acadians," the civilian said. He was wearing a cigarette in his mouth.

I recognized the voice right away. It belonged to René · Lévesque, bilingual CBC reporter and commentator. We shook hands.

"Yes, but this expulsion is different," I said. "It's English doing it to English."

"That's a nice change in Canada," he said.

"Maybe to try to even up the last one," I said. "So far, I haven't been able to find the name of a single French family in this expulsion."

"That's too bad," Lévesque said. "There goes my story." He shrugged and grinned.

"The people expelled from Gagetown weren't even a fifth column—like last time," I said.

"You read that in Haliburton," he said.

Good God, I thought, this guy reads more than press releases. He was right. I had read it in Thomas Haliburton's 1829 history of Nova Scotia.

Lévesque, like half-a-dozen other reporters, including me, was in Camp Gagetown to cover the week-long practice war of the 1st Canadian Infantry Division. It was the first divisional exercise at Gagetown. It was hard to take a great deal of interest in the 1st Division's manoeuvres against the army of "Fantasia," except, perhaps, for the day the Royal Canadian Air Force dropped a parachute company of Quebec's Royal 22nd Regiment in a stand of dead pine trees, causing spearing injuries but no deaths and prompting an apoplectic general (English-speaking) to shout up at the planes,

"What in God's name are you trying to do? Kill our only Frenchmen?"

I spent a lot of time poking around the back roads of the camp. I didn't realize anyone else might be doing the same. I guess I was conducting a lengthy memorial service to the farm in Jacksontown.

"Where are you headed now?" Lévesque asked.

"West Jerusalem," I said.

"I think I'll try Petersville," he said. "There's an old R-C church there and there might be a French name in the cemetery."

He shrugged. Was he serious? He kept a gentle needle in all the time. But he never jabbed viciously.

Besides the farms, the defence department had expropriated the few stores and blacksmith shops, the Jerusalem Telephone Company, Woods Lumber Company, 23 churches, 22 schools, eight public buildings (three agricultural society halls, three Orange lodges and two parish halls), and 27 cemeteries. Former area residents have been allowed to be—and sometimes are—buried in these graveyards; going home, so to speak. One Anglican church, St. Augustine's, was cut up in 1953 and re-assembled at Chipman.

There were two churches in Jerusalem, United and Baptist, the former with a parsonage and drive sheds. The paint was fast peeling from them but they were neat, clean and spare inside, the plain, hard pews awaiting congregations that would never return.

Jerusalem's early names were Sharp's Settlement, Mahood's Corner, Short's Corner, Barnett's Corner and then New Jerusalem. The "New" was eventually dropped, for convenience rather than any belief it had supplanted that other Jerusalem overseas. The hamlet is 10 miles from the St. John River and the first settlers came in on foot, a lucky few on horseback. They were mostly English, Scottish and Irish immigrants, with a sprinkling of United Empire Loyalists. The government supplied the first seed potatoes, oats and buckwheat (for the eternal morning pancakes). Horses gradually replaced oxen; and the mowing machine, reaper and thresher eventually took over from the sickle, scythe and flail. The first school opened in 1826, the first tavern in 1829. The first Baptist service was held in 1838 and a chapel built in 1856. The first Methodist church was established in 1841, the Sons of Temperance in 1855 and the post office in 1885. The telephone arrived in 1915 for 60 sub-scribers, and Loyal Orange Lodge No. 85, the Star of Jerusalem, was founded in 1926. The first snowplough didn't put in an appearance until 1946.

There were at least 16 other deserted hamlets in the camp. Polleyhurst, four miles west of Jerusalem, changed its name to West Jerusalem. Headline (named for a ridge, not a newspaper) became Coote Hill. Hamilton Mountain (850 feet), Armstrong's Corner, Petersville, North Clones, South Clones, Summer Hill, Hibernia, Lawfield, Inchby, Dunn's Corner, Olinville, Nerepis (always called Neverpiss in New Brunswick), Vincent and Shortholm all had their original names when they disappeared from county maps and the tax rolls.

I visited all or most of these vanishing places in the next few days. My army driver, Bill Saunders, came from Toronto. He rolled his eyes when I pointed to my map and put my finger on North Clones (there was a coalmine there that had served the locals only) or Nerepis (good for still another laugh) or Coote Hill. But he became interested in the cemeteries, wondering how old the graves were. Because the military were not permitted to enter the graveyards (there were big signs about that on all of them), Bill would ask me to slip in and check the oldest stones. I think the earliest I found was 1819, but we couldn't check them all. Many cemeteries we didn't see, or know about, because they were private ones at the far back corners of farms under a favorite oak, beech or pine.

Checking grave markers was the least I could do for Bill in return for his jeeping me over washboard roads and down rutted lanes to one more cluster of farm buildings.

"It's a shame, all this waste," Bill said one day. We were poking around a milk room that still had a sour smell. The winds blowing through the open door and smashed windows had not dispersed the odor three years later. There was a rusted cream separator still bolted to the floor.

"My nostalgia is getting to you," I said.

"Perhaps," Bill said. "It's easier to be nostalgic about this empty place than about Yonge and Bloor."

The 1st Division warriors laid on a night battle and we, were advised to observe from indoors rather than from a hedge, say, and risk getting run over by a tank. So a few of us moved into Dunn's Corner school for the night. First, in the twilight, I inspected Corbett's blacksmith shop nearby. Cinders from the forge were scattered about the dirt floor and the bellows had been slashed open (with a bayonet?). All the tools were gone except for a few broken tongs. Discarded horseshoes with bent nails in them formed a little heap in one corner.

The one-room school was a strong building that had apparently been rebuilt often and added to more than once. It sat in a half-acre of timothy, pitcher plant, jack-in-the-pulpit, lady's slipper, labrador tea and devil's-paint-brush. The two backhouses were still firmly in place and available for our use.

On one wall of the school, which seemed to have been behind the teacher's desk at one time, was the original blackboard—boards painted black, but the cracks now showing between them. A slate blackboard occupied the new end wall. Nothing had been left—no book, desk, chair, stove, child's slate or even a piece of chalk. The windows were partly boarded over. It was the only building I'd seen in the camp which somebody had tried to protect. A teacher or pupil with fond memories of Dunn's Corner? Perhaps a school trustee who didn't believe expropriation would stick.

It was a long night of noise, caused mainly by clanking tanks that got close enough to the school to tear big gaps in the fence surrounding it.

The farm buildings of Camp Gagetown didn't long endure the army and the weather. Nearly all of them were gone in 15 years. And by that time, the army didn't have enough troops to form a division and the purpose of the expropriation was lost. The camp now is rented to the United States National Guard for summer militia exercises.

I didn't see Lévesque again to speak with until the fall of 1986. I was in a long line of anglos outside a bookshop on Confederation Square in Ottawa on a cold November day. We were there to get Lévesque's autograph on his book, *Memoirs* (the English translation, of course). I waited for three-quarters of an hour, the only time I can remember being patient in a queue of whatever length. I had never lost my regard for Lévesque: an honest man fallen among mostly extremists, fools and bounders.

At last I reached the tiny table where Lévesque was signing furiously and chain-smoking at the same pace. His wispy little factotum-bodyguard stood looking out the window, also chain-smoking. Lévesque had a gracious word for everyone. He jumped up and shook hands with me as if he recognized me. He didn't, of course, 31 years later. I told him we'd been reporters at the same time in Gagetown decades ago, and he sat down promptly and wrote in his book: "A Dave McIntosh. Très cordial souvenirs de Gagetown. Salut. René Lévesque."

Despite his proud announcement, after a medical, that he had "the lungs of a baby," he died a year later, heralded and sung.

External Affairs Minister Paul Martin once gave me a pen he'd just used to sign a treaty but I lost it. I intend to hang on to my signed Lévesque book. That's only fair. I still have the cigars Pierre Trudeau handed me when his sons were born.

Unforgiveness

As I left for Hong Kong in 1966, I hoped that I'd have a longer stay there than I had had in 1950.

I flew to Tokyo in 1950 as a reporter to cover the early Canadian participation in the Korean war. I was the only passenger aboard the Royal Canadian Air Force North Star transport plane (propeller-driven), which was carrying a cargo of beer. In the Canadian military at least they have their priorities straight: first beer, then weapons.

I had watched the seaborne departure from Seattle, Washington, of the advance party of the Canadian Army contingent and reached Pusan, Korea, ahead of it to meet the same troops coming down the gangplank. During their passage, the Americans had pulled off an end run around the invading North Korean army, landing at Inchon in its rear, and the war appeared in the mopping-up stage—until the Chinese intervention. During the lull before the Chinese storm, I decided I should spend some time with the three-destroyer Canadian flotilla which was making our only significant military contribution in Korea. The only way I could get aboard was to join HMCS *Sioux* in Hong Kong, where she'd gone for some rest and repairs.

So I flew to Hong Kong by Canadian Pacific Airlines, relishing the prospect of at least a few days there before *Sioux* departed. I should have known the Canadian embassy in Tokyo would have the dates wrong. The moment I arrived at my hotel, there was a message that *Sioux* couldn't wait any longer—there was a war she was supposed to be engaged in—and she was making for sea, at that very hour, it so happened. I grabbed a taxi to the dockyard, hired a sampan and was hauled up the side of the destroyer in the stream as she began to put on speed. I threw some Japanese yen at the sampan. I hadn't had time even to change any money. Total elapsed time in Hong Kong was just under one hour.

The 1966 trip to Hong Kong, again undertaken as a reporter, had to do with the official Canadian observation of the 25th anniversary of the fall of the Hong Kong garrison at Christmas, 1941. The lebensraum-bound Japanese had cut up the Winnipeg Grenadiers and Quebec Royal Rifles and enslaved the survivors for the rest of the war. The delegation was made up of survivors of the survivors—that is, some of those who had come back alive in 1945 after the harsh beatings and the desperate lack of food and medicine in the Japanese prisoner-of-war camps. They all boarded the one plane in Ottawa, together with four or five reporters.

It was the most unnerving flight (not counting the war, when they were all unnerving) I was ever on, though that had nothing to do with the actual flying. The RCAF Yukon transport plane (again, propeller-driven) and its crew were perfectly dependable, as always, and the trip itself was uneventful.

It was the passengers.

There was something out of the ordinary about them, and not just that they had spent three-and-a-half years in prison camps. There was little talking among them, which struck me as strange when most of them hadn't seen each other for years, and some not since the war's end. There was something almost sinister in the way they looked at one another. And what talk there was seemed to be in whispers, so that conversations were limited to two men, heads close together, the rest temporarily ostracized. There was a pulse in the cabin, like electricity, or an artery.

I had tried to strike up conversation with a few of the men—that was my job—but all their words were vague, closed off, remote, ungrippable when, I thought, they should have been friendly and cheerful. A few men began to drink straight out of the bottles they had brought with them, but didn't pass them around.

I had been lucky enough to draw a seat beside Wilf Queen-Hughes, an editorial writer for the Winnipeg *Tribune* who had been a prisoner of the Japanese and, as a result, still had amoebic dysentery which sent him to the washroom every half hour or so, and not just on a plane.

Wilf and I exchanged the usual newspaper talk, which gradually branched out into more interesting subjects, such as his name. Wilf was years ahead of his time. His surname had been Hughes, he had married Gloria Queen, the daughter of the mayor of Winnipeg, and not only attached her surname to his but put it in front. It was a long time before I could ask him the question that was bothering me. Finally, I blurted it out:

"What in hell is going on in this airplane?"

"Hate," Wilf said. "Just sit and close your eyes. You can feel it, ricocheting around the cabin."

"Hate of what?" I asked.

"Each other. Well, maybe I'm exaggerating a bit, but not much. Hate between groups."

"Officers and men," I said. "There's nothing new about that in the military, though I've never felt it more strongly than I have here."

"No," Wilf said, "not necessarily officers and men. That comes into it in some cases, but it's not the main factor."

He paused, then said, "I guess it comes down to belief, in the religious sense. There were those in the prison camps who were, or at least tried to be, their brother's keeper, and there were those who looked after themselves and didn't give a damn about anybody else."

"But that's no different than life has ever been," I said, striking one of my profound notes.

"It's not the same as everyday life," Wilf said. "In the prison camps we were in, your life often depended on the guy next to you. And most often it depended on whether the guy who had managed to get hold of drugs would share them."

"This hate is about drugs?" I said.

"Drugs and food," he said. "Hundreds were dying of disease and malnutrition and overwork. In the malaria swamp, the man with the quinine is king."

From what I could make out, a great deal of the animosity shooting through the cabin seemed directed at a man sitting across the aisle from us and a couple of rows nearer the cockpit.

"What about that guy?" I asked Wilf. "It looks like hardly anybody will speak to him."

"You hit the king," he said. "Somehow he got his hands on most of the drugs that came into the camp. He hoarded them. He never gave any of them away, though they were meant for all of us. He sold some to a few cronies, but he kept the rest."

"He must have been an officer to be able to get his hands on the drugs in the first place," I said. Nobody was in uniform except one man, who was still in the army.

"He was," Wilf said.

We stopped to refuel in San Francisco and then headed for an overnight stay in Honolulu. By the time we were out over the Pacific, the passengers had sorted themselves into small huddles in which they talked vigorously, with extreme gestures towards and occasional curses about members of other groups. There were some who took no part in any of this, and I invited myself to a seat beside one of them. I told him that I felt there was a venom coursing through the plane.

"Yes," he said, "it's a shame. It's eating some of them up. Better they'd never organized this trip, or had let each man get there on his own."

"You seem to have kept away from it," I said.

"Well, it's perhaps hard to believe now but I prayed all the time I was in prison camp. I prayed in my bunk and in the Yokohama dockyard where I worked for a while and in the coalmine. I even prayed when a padre organized a service."

"God kept you alive?"

"Exactly," he said. "I was a believer before the war and I kept my faith, which seemed the best thing to do—the only thing to do—because there was nothing else to depend on. It gave me a great deal of comfort."

In all my years in the newspaper business, I'd never had an interview like this, not even with an Anglican primate.

"Did you pray for the others, too?"

"Of course," he said, looking at me strangely. "I even prayed for the Japanese."

"You've forgiven them, then?"

"Oh, yes. I forgave them at the time."

"You must be the only one in this plane."

"Oh, I don't think so. It's a funny thing, though, that the ones who hate seem to direct their hate against their former fellow prisoners instead of the Japanese. Maybe that's because they could forgive their enemies but not what their friends did to them."

Few would talk to me like Wilf and this man. Most would mention, awkwardly, the atrocities of their captors, especially the hideous beatings and, worse, the deliberate neglect of the sick and dying. They praised two men, both former officers, who had devoted themselves, day in and day out, to the relief of their companions' suffering and dismay. These two had kept up a constant stream of protest to the guards and thereby brought on themselves repeated beatings.

But only one or two switched talk from the behavior of the guards to what they saw as betrayal by fellow prisoners.

"That son of a bitch," one said, pointing to somebody far up the aisle, "the one with the white hair. He had a Jap guard who brought him vegetables from his garden. I don't know what he gave in return, cigarettes, or drugs, or money—or information about the rest of us. It was a lack of vegetables which helped ruin our health. He ate them all himself, at night. We could hear him crunching away. I'll never forget that sound."

After a moment, he added, "Why didn't we beat hell out of him? Why don't we do it now, come to think of it?"

I went back to Wilf with more questions.

"How are these men so sure that so-and-so hoarded the drugs or informed on them or got more than their fair share?"

"They aren't," Wilf said. "But terrible things happened and somebody has to be blamed. It's been festering away for twenty years and now we'll never know the truth. It's like the government—it never really wanted to know what went on in the Japanese camps. They might have to do something about it, like giving us a proper pension, or asking Japan for compensation. They even hid their eyes from the war crimes trials and pretended that only Americans and Australians and some Dutchmen were affected."

I said I was surprised that apparently no revenge had been taken on the hoarders and collaborators.

Wilf said he had heard of three cases, but had sketchy details on only one.

"There was a junior officer, a Canadian, who went to live in England after the war. He had been a particular bastard in one camp, hoarding drugs and swapping them for the food ration of dying men. He was hunted down by fellow prisoners, I don't know how many. It took them about two years. They got him outside a pub in London one night and beat him to death in an alley. They kicked him into a pulp. No one was ever arrested and, of course, I don't know for sure that it was former POWs who did it. From what I read in the London papers at the time, the police thought he had been rolled by some punks. But everybody who had been in that camp knew that a score had been paid off."

Wilf said he had heard of a similar case in Australia and of another in San Diego in 1945 when a returning POW had been stabbed to death the same day his repatriation ship had docked.

Wilf didn't discuss with me any of the details of his life in prison camp. "You can see the results," he said, as he left his seat on one of his regular visits to the washroom. He didn't seem to harbor any hate for fellow prisoners who had cheated others out of drugs and food, and, in some cases, their lives. But he wasn't tolerant, either.

"I'm surprised they'd come on this trip," he said. "They know that we know. Perhaps they think the rest of us have forgotten. If they do, they'll know differently by the end of this visit, if not already."

He reflected a moment, and added, "Worst of all, of course, is that maybe they just don't give a damn. Up you, Jack, I'm all right."

On the next long haul to our Wake Island stop-over (I wrote a too-clever-by-half piece beginning, "Wake Island is for sleeping"), I made an accidental discovery from a former sergeant: the external affairs department in Ottawa and Tokyo had made the arrangements for accommodation for the veterans in Hong Kong, and all former officers were to stay in the posh Peninsula Hotel and all the former other ranks in Stanley barracks, the very buildings in which they had been held prisoner by the Japanese in 1941. I wrote a story about that, too, and filed it to my office from Wake. By the time we reached Hong Kong, reservations for the other ranks had been switched to the Peninsula or other hotels.

When the veterans arrived in Tokyo for a ceremony at the Yokohama War Cemetery where many of the Canadians from the slave camps are buried, a senior official of the external affairs department greeted me at the plane.

"Well," he said, "you've certainly caused us a lot of trouble."

A Prairie Conversation

The bus pulled into the farmyard and spilled its contents—reporters, photographers, cameramen and major and minor factoti of the Conservative party—into the warm Saskatchewan sun.

Conservative leader Robert Stanfield had come to see what a big (7,700 acres) prairie wheat farm looked like and maybe to pick up some ideas on how the West might get rid of its stack of 900 million bushels of unsold wheat.

There were just a few days more than a month before the federal general election on June 25, and Stanfield, like the other party leaders, was trying to cram in as much Canadian geography as possible before his ballot date with Prime Minister Pierre Trudeau and Tommy Douglas, the New Democratic Party leader.

The morning of the farm visit, Stanfield had done some mainstreeting in Yorkton and then gone on to the Legion hall at Melville, where he told a noontime gathering, "I'm not a farm expert." Well, that was allowable, I supposed; he came from a long line of underwear makers in Nova Scotia.

Lorlie, on the road from Melville to Fort Qu'Appelle and Regina, is so small that it had failed to make the new gazeteer of Saskatchewan, published in Saskatoon that very year, though Lilac, with 13 residents, had made it.

The bus ride had been a diversion, partly because of the scenery (I relish the immensity of the plains), partly because it was a nice change from a plane, but mostly because I'd been lucky enough to grab a seat beside E.A. Goodman, the Conservative national campaign chairman. Goodman never deserved his press nickname, Fast Eddie. He sometimes gave the air (on purpose) of being the backest of the back-room boys, but he was too up-front to fool anyone. He had a huge fund of current political stories and anecdotes and believed in sharing them. He was a delight to listen to, which is more, a lot more, than you can say for most politicians.

"Are you going to sweep all the Saskatchewan seats like you did in 1965?" I asked Goodman between stories.

"Naw," he said.

"How many?" I asked.

"We'll be lucky to take half of them," he said.

Fine way for the national campaign chairman to be talking, but Goodman couldn't help himself. That's what happens when you're honest and straightforward. (The Conservatives won five of 13 Saskatchewan seats, one fewer than the New Democratic Party. The Liberals took two.)

Goodman was one of the precious few holdovers from the glorious days (for reporters) of the John Diefenbaker campaigns. Alas, they were gone forever. No more campaign trains, the great man shaking hands ("Good to see *you*") up and down the platform at a hundred whistlestops, verbally and happily jousting with interlopers at the big-city evening rallies. Now there were the interminable plane flights, direct, it seemed, from shopping centre to shopping mall. We reporters sensed that the political age of the scheduled visit with photo opportunity and the television clip with the rehearsed spontaneous quote was upon us. Goodbye town hall heckle, hello laugh track. So long voter, come aboard, pollster.

Here in Saskatchewan, Stanfield would have to look particularly knowledgeable, especially to farmers, if he was going to persuade Conservatives that the party had done the right thing the previous year by ditching the Old Chief. Saskatchewan had been Diefenbaker's stumping ground during all those lean years, when, as he said himself, the only protection afforded Conservatives was the province's game laws, and in the fat prime ministerial years afterwards.

Stanfield was introduced to the farmer, John Stilborn, then went over to one of the red-painted dwarf silos used to store surplus grain and let some of the unmarketed wheat run through his fingers. This photo opportunity did not work out well, however (wheat is a poor prop unless it's standing in a field), and the newspapers next day all used the result of the earlier photo op at Melville: Stanfield in a railroader's cap. Without hats or placards, the cameras dry up.

Once wheat-through-the-fingers was done with, the press drifted away and began asking one another how far it was to Regina and would there be time for a couple of drinks before the evening rally there.

This subject interested me, too, but I decided that my immediate duty, as representative of omnipresent Canadian Press, was to stick with Stanfield and Stilborn, or Bob and Jack as I came to think of them during the next awful 20 minutes.

Bob and Jack walked away from the storage bins and towards an open field and I trailed along, hoping to catch Stanfield's response to Stilborn's proposals for handling the wheat overload. Stilborn was a director of the Saskatchewan Wheat Pool and thus a farmer of some influence and savvy. He also had some pretty definite ideas on the need for payments to farmers for wheat stored on their farms. He spoke at some length at first, Stanfield nodding at the end of every other sentence. Stilborn was advising immediate subsidies to keep up production until world markets for wheat improved. Ninety percent of farmers had to sell their entire produce each year to remain solvent, he said.

Stilborn looked at Stanfield, waiting for a reply.

Stanfield didn't say anything.

I moved closer, ear and notebook poised, so that we formed a tight-knit trio on the rim of the sunny prairie.

Still Stanfield didn't say anything. I was embarrassed at the silence, and for Stilborn.

Finally, I decided to break the impasse.

"How's the growing weather been?" I asked brightly.

"Just like today," Stilborn said.

"No drought like the thirties?" I said.

"Not since the thirties," Stilborn said.

Ask him when he planted, I silently ordered Stanfield. Stanfield said nothing.

"Do you plant in the fall?" I asked.

"Mostly," Stilborn said.

"Red Fife?" I asked. I'd read that in a Ralph Connor or Nellie McClung novel or something like that borrowed from the Haskell Free Library at home when I was a boy.

"Red Fife went out at the turn of the century," Stilborn said.

"Yes, of course," I said. "I meant Marquis."

"That's long gone, too," Stilborn said.

I screamed silently at Stanfield: ask him what he plants now.

Stanfield looked interested but didn't open his mouth. How could he have gotten this far in politics without any small talk?

By this time, Stilborn seemed aware that all I was trying to do was to get the Conservative leader engaged in conversation, any conversation. I'd already used up three subjects: weather, the dirty thirties and wheat varieties.

Stilborn looked amused, but he didn't help. Why should he? He was a farmer. I was Mr. Interlocutor. There was a long pause. We all looked down at the ground and scuffed our shoes in it, as if we were about to turn over a few diamonds.

"I notice you don't have many cattle barns," I said at last.

"That's right," Stilborn said, his eyes twinkling. "But it's only because we don't have any cattle."

Stanfield chuckled at that, but he didn't offer any wisdom of his own. He appeared perfectly content to let me carry the ball.

My summers on a New Brunswick potato farm in the early 1930s didn't fit me for a talk on the husbandry of Saskatchewan, but I plunged on.

"I see you don't grow any potatoes," I said inanely.

"No, we buy our potatoes at the store," Stilborn said.

"Ontario potatoes?"

"I guess so," Stilborn said. "I've never thought to ask."

I thought that my mention of a Maritimes farm product might spur Stanfield to join in the profound exchange between Stilborn and me. Nothing doing. I tried again.

"I used to stook wheat on my uncle's farm in New Brunswick," I said, heavily emphasizing New Brunswick. I was trusting that Stanfield knew that New Brunswick was Nova Scotia's neighbor.

"I've seen pictures of hand-stooking, but I've never stooked myself," Stilborn said. "We go from combine to truck."

"Of course," I said.

"How many acres of wheat did your uncle have?" Stilborn asked. I guessed he'd given up on Stanfield, too.

"Ten," I said.

Stilborn whistled. "That many?" he said.

Ask him how many acres he has, I shouted silently at Stanfield. I already knew. It was in Stanfield's itinerary handed to the press that morning. But Stanfield wasn't to be drawn in.

There was another long pause before I tried another tack.

"Mr. Stilborn," I said, "I think you've explained to Mr. Stanfield the need for advance payments on farm-stored grain. What has been his reaction?"

Stilborn's eyebrows shot up. "You'd better ask him," he said. "He's right here."

"What is your reaction to Mr. Stilborn's recommendations?" I asked.

I waited. My God, Stanfield was going to speak.

"Well, I'm no farm expert," Stanfield said. "Maybe you'd better ask Alvin Hamilton."

Hamilton had been Diefenbaker's agriculture minister and was travelling with Stanfield that very day. But there was no way I was going to ask Alvin Hamilton a question on wheat. I'd get a minimum two-hour lecture. I suddenly recalled a story about a prairie funeral. An awkward silence at the graveside was finally broken when one farmer stepped forward and said, "If nobody has anything else to say, I'd like to say a few words about wheat."

"I think I should hear the party's wheat policy from the leader rather than from Mr. Hamilton," I said stiffly.

"Well . . . "

My God, Stanfield was getting ready to speak again.

"Well, maybe I'll have something to say on that tonight in Regina," Stanfield said. He paused, then added, "If Alvin has it ready in time."

He meant it as a joke. Stilborn didn't laugh either.

"Well . . . " Stanfield began.

Surely not a third speech, I said to myself.

"Well, I guess we'd better be going," Stanfield said. "Thank you for your hospitality, Mr. Stilwell."

"Stilborn," Stilborn said.

"Yes," Stanfield said. "I've learned a great deal."

We strolled back to the farmhouse, where Mrs. Stanfield was chatting vigorously with the other members of the Stilborn family.

"Get anything?" a colleague asked me.

"The whole Tory wheat policy," I said.

"Yeah," he said.

We got back on the bus and I sat down again beside Eddie Goodman.

"Why in hell didn't you rescue me by leaving earlier?" I demanded. I explained what had not happened.

"You read the itinerary," Goodman said. "Twenty minutes for conversation with Mr. Stilborn. Twenty minutes allotted, twenty minutes spent. That's why I'm campaign chairman." He guffawed.

That night, in Regina, Stanfield outlined some complex formula for minimum wheat payments tied to production costs and adjustable after one year. Nobody in the hall understood it except Alvin Hamilton. But I was the only reporter to have the inside information on how the formula was arrived at through intense negotiations in a farmyard at Lorlie, Saskatchewan.

Squirrel in the Road

The liquor store in Havelock is handy for the traveller because it's right on No. 7 highway. Jean and I were driving from Ottawa to Toronto on No. 7, as we used to do, and stopped at the liquor store for a bottle of rum.

I pulled out onto the highway again and drove only a few yards when I saw a squirrel on the road in front of me. It seemed to be moving, but wasn't. Then I saw it was trying to move, but couldn't. Its hindquarters had been hit and crushed, and the squirrel was trying to drag itself off the road by its front legs. It strained with its two good legs and shoulders, its head upright, but couldn't free its wounded parts from the tar.

I steered around the squirrel. Then I thought, I can't leave it like that.

"I've got to go back," I said.

"One bottle will do for now," Jean said. She hadn't seen the squirrel.

"It's not that," I said, and explained.

"Yes," she said, simply.

I went around the block and came out on the highway again. The squirrel was still struggling to move its crushed hindquarters.

"I can't look," Jean said.

I drove slowly, lining up the left front wheel to put the creature out of its agony.

I felt or heard—perhaps I only imagined that I felt or heard—a tiny crunch.

Just then, I looked to my left. A car coming from the opposite direction now was just abreast of us. The woman driver was looking at me in a mixture of horror and contempt.

Of course, she couldn't know. But I still see that accusing face, even though I've stopped going through Havelock. Now I cut south to 401 at Tweed on No. 38.

Chicken Macdonalds

Even on a sunny day, Culloden Moor is a loathsome place, dank, evil.

I walked it with my wife on a bright day in May (we had had nine consecutive cloudless days, a glory unknown previously in Scotland in this century), and I didn't entertain such dark thoughts at first. After all, the Battle of Culloden had been fought 236 years before. What could an ancient royalist rivalry between Scots and English possibly mean to two Canadians who chanced to bear Scottish names? (Jean is a MacKinnon.)

But Culloden is insidious. We walked across what had been the English lines to the centre of Highland Scotland's ragged front, held that awful day of April 16, 1746, by Clan Chattan, mainly the Mackintoshes, led by Alexander MacGillivray of Dunmaglass. Here ended in dreadful carnage the 1745 rising of Bonnie Prince Charlie, still referred to in Scotland as "the 'forty-five," the final conquest of the Celtic Scot by the Anglo-Saxon.

There is a large, round stone cairn near the centre of the battlefield, and scattered about are small, rough stones marking the graves of the clansmen, here the Mackintoshes, there the Frasers, Macleans, Stewarts, Farquharsons, MacLachlans, Chisholms, Grants and, by the Well of the Dead, the brave MacGillivray. It is all vainglorious and sad.

There was an old Highland custom that when clansmen were summoned to battle, each brought to the rallying place a stone which he added to the heap brought by the others. After the battle, each survivor carried away a stone from this rough cairn, and the stones remaining gave a wordless toll of casualties. This was not done at Culloden, and there was no battlefield memorial of any kind for more than a century. The Scots were not allowed to build one; the English were too ashamed. In 1858, a cairn was begun but never finished. The present one was built in 1881 by the Gaelic Society of Inverness, which conducts an annual remembrance ceremony.

I began to read the booklet Jean had bought in the modest, white-washed building run by the Scottish National Trust. It said the English commander, the fat (252 pounds) Duke of Cumberland, son of King George II, had all the Scottish prisoners and wounded clubbed or bayoneted to death, or burned alive. His army pillaged, raped and murdered the five miles to Inverness. Women and children were killed, the Prince's supporters hanged without trial. And that was just a foretaste of the terror, fire and sword visited on the Highlands. They didn't catch Charlie, though.

By this time, I was getting pretty worked up. Then we saw the Trust's short film on the 'forty-five. It ended with more references to English butchery. I rushed from the little theatre, looking for a dirty limey to throttle.

"What are you going to do, start the eighty-two?" asked my wife, whose mother was a MacGillivray, for heaven's sake.

My brother, who had visited Culloden a few years earlier, hadn't filled me in on the English cutthroats, among them General James Wolfe, who relished the slaughter, and who conquered Montcalm on Quebec's Plains of Abraham with (I hate to say it) the Fraser Highlanders, only 13 years later. I guess my brother was too upset about what he found out about the Macdonalds. All he said was, "No wonder there are so few MacIntoshes today and so many Macdonalds. We were in the centre, charged and were wiped out. The Macdonalds were on the left and ran away."

Macdonald historians are still trying to cover this up, but I know my brother is right: he got it from the chief himself, the Mackintosh of Mackintosh, at the clan seat nearby. There are no Macdonald grave markers at Culloden, except maybe way off in the woods.

I managed to simmer down after a while, and we drove on to Fort George on Moray Firth. It was built soon after Culloden to help prevent any further Highland rebellions. It is still occupied by British troops and its ancient cannons are still aimed at Inverness, capital of the Highlands.

We moved on to Cawdor Castle, also near Culloden, still lived in, and lavishly: acres of putting-green lawn, snipped hedges, immaculate gardens, splendid furniture, tapestried walls, moat, drawbridge, dungeon, castle keep—the works.

Our admission fee to this splendor was $3.35 each. The castle is a money-maker for its private owner, while the Scottish National Trust lives hand to mouth on charity and can barely keep a tatty patch of grass mown around the Culloden cairn and the Well of the Dead.

It wasn't until we were leaving the castle that I discovered that Cawdor is a sept of Clan Campbell, and that the castle's owner-occupant was Lord Campbell.

The Campbells fought on the English side at Culloden. Well, they didn't really fight. They knocked breaches in stone fences so that the English cavalry could pour through unopposed and annihilate the unprotected Scottish right flank, then followed stealthily to slay the wounded remnant.

"Do you want to look at the Campbell tartans in the gift shop before we go?" my wife said.

I glared at her and stamped out over the drawbridge, all the while expecting a Campbell gillie to pour boiling oil on us from the battlement.

Gravel Cookies

Most places don't live up to your expectations. Most people don't, either, but this is about places.

The Leaning Tower of Pisa leans all right, but it's in a grubby little town and you have to crane your neck up close. I've been to London lots of times but could never be bothered to see its Tower; it's too out of the way. The Acropolis is okay, but its environs have been trampled flat and hard by countless visiting feet. Fouquet's in Paris is very swish, but it rained the day I had an exquisite Dover sole there. The Taj Mahal is magnificent, but to see it at its best you should go in moonlight; I did, and barked my shins in the poor light. Borobudur on the island of Java is only a little less magnificent, but I became dehydrated in the heat climbing its stone terraces and had to lie down for a couple of hours with a salt pill. San Francisco is attractive, but the cable car bell woke me from a nap at the Fairmont. Bellapais Abbey in Cyprus is restful and serene, but the road to it off the Nicosia-Kyrenia highway is much too narrow. The Peninsula in Hong Kong is one of the world's great hotels, but the last time I was there it took them all of 15 minutes to invisible-mend my torn jacket.

But, you will be relieved to know, there are two places in the world that didn't disappoint me when, after years of yearning, I finally reached them. One is the Great Pyramid of Cheops near Cairo, the other Dawson, Yukon Territory.

Dawson, as much as Cheops, represents a lost civilization. I dare say that the men who moiled for gold on the Klondike are as far removed from us as the men who pushed and pulled Cheops' huge blocks of stone into geometric place. But I imagine that Dawson was by far the happier place.

In the summer of 1982, three officials of the Customs department of the ministry of national revenue were to inspect all Canadian Customs posts on the border between Yukon-British Columbia and Alaska. At the last minute, one of them couldn't go, and I was invited in his place. I jumped at the chance, mostly because I wanted to go and partly because I was writing a history of Customs at the time and had just reached the most interesting part: establishment of Customs posts in the Chilkoot and White Passes at the start of the Klondike gold rush. Robert W. Service, here I come.

We flew to Whitehorse and, accompanied by two local officers, drove by van for nearly two weeks through the western Yukon, northwestern British Columbia and eastern Alaska.

"Will we see any moose?" Roger wanted to know as we left Whitehorse early one morning for the long drive to Dawson. Roger was one of the Ottawa officials.

"Herds of them," said Terry, the local manager.

As it turned out, we saw one, from afar, on our last day, and Roger complained to Terry, "From what you said, I thought we were going to have to shoot our way through."

But the delight for me that final day was not only seeing the moose, but seeing it on the very shore of the lake (Tagish) where Customs officer John Godson in 1897 waded out in hip boots from his tent to collect duties from boats carrying American goods headed for the Klondike.

In the Yukon, you don't pass up one gas station with the airy thought, Oh, I'll stop at the next one. There often isn't a next one until long after you've run out of gas. We left the Alaska Highway near Lake Laberge and I began to recite "The Cremation of Sam McGee." To my disgust, all four others in the van knew the words and joined in, ruining my expected solo turn.

From the lake, we headed north and west into the wide interior valley that carries the Yukon River and many of its tributaries. Long drives apart lie Carmacks, Pelly Crossing, Stewart Crossing—old but still rude settlements whose garages and gas pumps make them important. The immense scrub forests (effectively hiding herds of moose) close in on both sides of the gravel highway, but the roadside fireweed, wild rose, Arctic lupin, sky pilot, mountain bluebell and jacob's ladder bloom through the dust like beacons in a fog.

At last, Flat Creek, where the road joins the Klondike River, which soon meets the Yukon at Dawson. All along the Klondike are the seried tailings, like huge gravel cookies, and ancient dredges, like beached dinosaurs, left from the old gold diggings. It was here, on August 17, 1896, that George W. Carmack and his two partners,

Skookum Jim and Tagish Charlie, struck it rich before rushing down the Yukon River to Forty-Mile to register their claim four days later. For the Indians, the Klondike had always been a salmon river, and they used to dry their fish on the flats at the confluence of the Klondike and Yukon where Dawson was built. Joseph Ladue, a prescient prospector and trader, staked the townsite in the very month that the big strike was made. Two years later, at the height of the Klondike rush, the population was 16,000. The city is named after G.W. Dawson, director of the Geological Survey of Canada, who led an expedition into the district in 1877. Dawson was the Yukon's capital until 1953 when, its gold largely played out, the seat of government was shifted to busier Whitehorse. In 1981, the residents of Dawson numbered 697.

For me, Dawson still lives and breathes 1898. Not even the ersatzness concocted for the tourists put me off. (The bar in the Eldorado Hotel where I stayed is called the Sluice Box Lounge; in a modern sluice box beside a souvenir shop on Bonanza Creek, the tourist can swirl his pan of pre-goldened gravel to find a microscopic fleck of yellow.) My ardor for the boardwalk street, the falsefront buildings and the empty wharf was undampened. It was all just as I had imagined from my boyhood study of Jack London, James Oliver Curwood, Charlie Chaplin, Nelson Eddy and, of course, Robert W. Service. I believed.

And it would have been easy to be disillusioned. The restored Palace Grand Theatre was staging the most boring production in the history of the Yukon, or any other territory. The Palace audience is captive, the theatre being part of the tour package for mainly oldsters (most of them widows) who flow through the Yukon and Alaska every summer for a change of scenery from the Florida and California packages.

The evening I attended the Palace Grand ($7.50 a seat), a couple with more courage than I tried to escape the tedium by bolting out of one of the emergency exits at the side of the theatre. Up in Dawson, the sun stays up nearly all night, and the weather forecasts say things like "sunny tonight." The sun poured like a crucible through the open side door, blotting out the stage lighting and blinding the fleeing couple and the rest of us, still timidly seated. The pair groped their way out through the fierce glare and managed to shut the door with a bang that would easily have drowned out all the evening's applause put together. We had to adjust again to the semi-darkness of the interior, and the purported play, unfortunately, continued.

The presentation was called *The Truth Will Out*, billed as a musical melodrama. It had absolutely nothing to do with the Yukon, or Canada. It was a Victorian yawner which must have put even the Victorians to sleep. We couldn't sleep because when the Canadian government restored the Palace Grand in 1962, one of the heritage touches applied was a return to the wooden, upright chairs. The cast of seven didn't know how to play the piece for the three potential laughs in it. The longed-for intermission after the first excruciating act (one more was threatened) permitted the playgoers to depart stealthily, which most of us did. The sunlight was still dazzling when we stumbled outside. Good. The cast would not be afforded cover of darkness on their way home.

While tourists are being misled to the Palace Grand, the locals repair to Diamond-Tooth-Gertie's gambling hall: two-dollar membership fee, booze, cancan girls, blackjack, roulette, crown-and-anchor, and Texas seven-card poker (five in front of the dealer, two down to each of the 12 players.) You don't need more than two seconds in the Palace Grand and Diamond-Tooth-Gertie's to determine which crowd is having the happier time. It's Diamond-Tooth like a royal flush over a pair of treys.

Only a couple of stretches of boardwalk separate the two establishments. In 1981, Dawson ripped out its old boardwalks to make way for new planks. But financing became a problem and new boardwalks were episodic around town, although there were enough of them to wipe your feet on rainy days before you hit another plankless section of mud.

Gertie's was going full blast when I arrived with fellow refugees from the Palace Grand. The hall is as big as a small hangar, with a modest stage at the far end. The games of chance are arranged along the walls and up the centre, and there is a large alcove for the poker players, who are allowed only the one style, Texas. Drinks are served by waitresses at large who are permitted no cleavage. The biggest chip in play seemed to be a green 25-dollar one. I bought a few purples at a dollar each, but the black 29 refused to come up on the roulette wheel and I settled for some beer. Singing Gertie and the cancans were performing four times a night (day, really). They were dressed almost as decorously as the waitresses and the act would have passed muster in a Methodist Sunday school in 1900. Only the passers-through like me gawked even briefly at the show. The rest all bent to their work over the gaming tables. The biggest bet I saw on the poker table was 10 dollars, very big-time for someone like me used to 10-cents-and-a-quarter-on-the-last-card.

Chips, whether for gambling, beer, liquor or food, were the only currency in circulation in the hall. The women with the groaning beer trays were usually tipped a purple chip while the dealer at the poker table usually received a five-dollar chip from the winner, which he tucked into his shirt pocket under his black vest. At one point, a player sharply questioned the dealer; the dealer explained quietly; the questioner nodded acquiescence. I waited in vain for somebody to kick over the table and start blasting.

Two uniformed but hatless Mounties paid a social call, chatting up the locals, some of them miners still working Klondike creeks for a bare living, but mostly hotel and motel operators and souvenir shop owners financially better off, at least in summer. The hall closed at 2 a.m. Nobody had been asked to leave, let alone bounced. It was still broad daylight. (Every June 21, hundreds drive up to the peak of 2,900-foot Midnight Dome, behind the town, to see the sun not set over the Ogilvie Range.)

The public library is above the liquor store. It is open Sundays from 2 to 9 p.m. The liquor store is not open Sunday at all. Dawson has had a museum since 1901, past and present going hand in hand.

But the chief shrine, of course, is Robert W. Service's two-room log cabin. There I found a young man dressed in early 1900s clothes (except for the Adidas), rocking on the porch and reading aloud passages from a modern edition of Service's collected poems. Many tourists recited the words from memory right along with him. I was a bit put out because the young man looked suspiciously like one of the purported actors at the Palace Grand.

One is permitted to look into the great man's cabin through a roped doorway. Visitors used to be allowed in, but the artifacts began disappearing. The tin-facade Bank of Commerce on the riverfront, where Service used to work, is still in business. (Banks last longer than gold.) The old assay office above the bank can still be seen, though the gold is fake.

Jack London's Klondike cabin had been reconstructed on a patch of weeds near Service's cabin but, when I was there, it was bare; the floor was dirt and being used as a garbage receptacle by passers-by. Which may prove that when Canadians are given the choice, they opt for Canadian culture.

There are dilapidated buildings here and there all over town, especially near the waterfront in the old commercial section, and they give Dawson a dishevelled, if not ramshackle appearance. There is no disposition to have the false-front eyesores torn down. They lean over the street in drunken disorder, the Occidental Hotel, Ruby's Place, Billy Biggs' Great Northern Hotel and the others, patiently awaiting a day of restoration. Parks Canada is doing what it can, and so are the Yukon government and the historical society. But the work is painfully slow, and signs giving notice that buildings will be restored have long been overgrown with weeds.

The best-kept property is the early North West Mounted Police cemetery partway up Midnight Dome. Wild roses bloom on the graves and the original wooden headboards are kept freshly white-painted, the black lettering standing out as starkly as a red tunic against the Yukon sky.

An Indian fish factory, staked out by a franco trader, endowed by an anglo prospector, fabled for gambling, booze, Mounties and gold, and enshrined by its very own poet—Dawson is about as Canadian as you can get.

War's
Leftovers

In 1945, when the war ended, I decided to write a book about my knee-knocking air force experiences while they were still fresh in my mind. (I needn't have worried—they still are.) The next year, I actually started the writing, but didn't get far. I was too busy being a reporter.

I began thinking about a book again in 1953 when I was sent to England to help cover the coronation of Queen Elizabeth II. My last wartime airfield was at Hunsdon, a village no more than 30 miles north of London. I called up the air ministry one day to ask whether the field was still in use and, if so, whether I might get in for a look-'round. The ministry said, five days later, that it had no record of Hunsdon; it must have been abandoned.

I got off the train at St. Margarets on a Sunday morning and walked two-and-a-half miles east to Hunsdon, a cluster of houses where three roads meet. Turn right before the pub, a short stretch, and there at the now unfenced entrance was the old guardhouse, full of bags of fertilizer.

The road to the control tower was overgrown but the ruts showed signs of farm use. The tower had governed all the goings and comings of our squadron's Mosquito planes, mostly at night. Nearly every pane of glass was smashed by postwar rocks and unmilitary bullets, and the concrete walls were gashed and chipped. Only a few flakes of paint remained, but in the stairwell to the second floor I could still make out traces of letters of a huge, red-painted QUIET. I climbed the glass-strewn cement stairs to the large room that had housed the controller and his staff. All the equipment was gone, of course: the receivers, transmitters, microphones, telephones and assorted black boxes. I spotted on the floor one empty cartridge from a Very pistol. The window running the length of the side of the tower overlooking the aerodrome had vanished, allowing the weather to pour in. Outside the empty frame was the concrete catwalk that permitted the controller to see a wider and clearer horizon. One night in November, 1944, Sid, who was my pilot, and I had sat in this humming, faintly lit room for four hours waiting for word whether Jack and George would make it back from Germany. They wouldn't.

The iron fence along the catwalk had been torn away, but I stepped out into the sunlight momentarily. All around the control tower were gently waving fields of hay, corn and buckwheat. The operations room, where we navigators had plotted our night raids (on Germany, and on pubs in nearby towns), had been ploughed under, along with all the other wooden buildings except two primitive hangars that now contained baled hay and machinery, including a combine. The horseshoe-shaped earthen aircraft bays, thrown up to protect our planes from bomb blast, had been levelled to ease the way for harrow, seeder and cultivator. The sergeants' mess and movie house were now the home of Herts Pharmaceuticals Ltd.

I went down the control tower steps, as I had that November night in 1944, thinking guiltily that though I felt bad about Jack and George, better them than me. I walked through hip-high timothy to the intersection of the two runways. I startled two grouse, which whirred away, and a small deer, which bolted down the north-south runway and into a clump of trees.

Weeds and twitch grass had sprouted through cracks in the runways and the perimeter track. There were skid marks on the east end of the east-west runway which were too narrow to have been made by the tires of 418 Squadron's Mosquitos, and I learned later that the runway was used sometimes as a car race track.

I stood where the two runways crossed and looked around, the only figure in that green, rippling landscape. Perhaps it had all been worthwhile: a military airfield had been turned into a farm. I had been far too scared flying over Germany to have helped make the slightest contribution to our side (perhaps, at least, I had not helped theirs). And anyway, my pilot had contributed more than enough for both of us. But I knew I had been on the right side and that I wasn't ashamed of having been there. Perhaps I can express what I felt by quoting Henry V's Shakespearean exhortation on the field of Agincourt and by substituting only one word, which you'll be able to detect right off:

And gentlemen in Canada, now abed,
Shall think themselves accursed they were not here.

I walked down the runway in our old takeoff direction (east to west) to the remains of the perimeter track and past the guardhouse for the last time. I was soon at our favorite wartime pub, Ye Olde Turkey Cock.

I stepped in the door hesitantly. There was the publican's wife behind the bar in the familiar spot she had occupied when Canadian airmen were the chief patrons. She looked up and said, "Good afternoon, Mr. McIntosh. Brown ale?"

I knew I'd been a frequent customer of the Turkey Cock, but never had realized before how frequent.

"Yes, please," I managed to blurt out after her stunning performance in pulling a name out of a nine-year-old hat.

"How did you do that, Mrs. er, ah?" I asked.

"Green. Oh, it's quite easy. There are only two necessary ingredients. The customer has to be a regular—that was you, all right—and always have the same drink. When I think McIntosh—and I haven't for a long time, mind you—I don't think toffee, but instead brown ale. And when I think brown ale, I think McIntosh."

She offered her hand, laughing, and called her husband over. He shook hands, too, but not as warmly as she had. He probably still hadn't got over having a pubful of drunken Canadians night after night, his premises awash in beer, glasses crashing, lewd songs drowning out all decent conversation, his village regulars more and more irritated and disconsolate.

I bought the landlord and his wife a drink and offered one to an elderly man standing next to me at the bar.

"No thank you," he said brusquely. I was taken aback; I'd never known an Englishman to decline a drink.

"Perhaps I should explain," he said, politeness creeping into his voice. "During the war, we had to stand outside the pub just to wait for an empty glass, let alone anything in it. Then we had to fight our way in to get close enough to the bar to get the dirty glass filled."

"What if I handed you a dirty glass now?" I asked. "Would that do it?"

He laughed. But he still said no.

"How's business?" I asked Mrs. Green.

"Oh, it slumped dreadfully after you Canadians left —thank heaven," she said. "Now we can keep the bar wiped off and dry. There's very little breakage except sometimes on Saturday night. And, if I may say so, no sick to slip in on the walk outside."

"Were we really that bad?" I asked. (I knew we were, and probably worse.)

"Yes," she said, "but there were redeeming qualities."

"Such as?"

"Well, you never haggled and you never sneaked out without paying."

"That's right," Mr. Green chimed in. "We had to worry about the furniture and the glasses, but never about anybody not paying." He reflected a moment. "Actually, you usually overpaid," he said.

"That's because we never understood the money, even after years over here," I said.

"You Canadians never took any interest in the money at all until it got to a five-pound note," he said. "Up to that point, you just put down handfuls of coins and wads of one-pound and ten-shilling notes on the bar."

"Where they'd become sopping wet," Mrs. Green said. "We'd try to smooth out the notes before we put them in the till. By the end of the evening, the till was half full of beer, too. We'd have to swab it out."

"And sometimes my wife would iron crumpled notes when she was doing the laundry," he said, topping up my glass of nut-brown ale.

If the English had wanted uncrumpable paper currency they should have used their toilet paper.

"Maybe the squadron can have a reunion here one day," I said. It would be awkward, with no hotel.

"That would be nice," the landlord said. "Perhaps you could drive up from London for an afternoon." Just the thought of our squadron spending a whole evening in his pub struck terror in his heart.

"I must go look at the house where I lived," I said.

"Oh, it's lovely now," Mrs. Green said. "Completely restored."

I left on that cheery sally and took the road to the south side of the field. I found the house, at the end of the lane, where a dozen of us had slept. I had a hard time recognizing it, though I knew I had the right place because the lane ended in a footbridge across a brook. The debris had been cleared away and the brook was running again. The house had been painted, the flag-stones reset, the hedges trimmed, the trees pruned, the lawn cut and the flowers replanted. The windows were open, and pretty curtains rustled in them on all three floors. When we'd been there, the grounds had been unkempt and overgrown, the unheated rooms dreary behind their blacked-out windows, a sallowness over-hanging the house. At least we'd kept it in restorable condition.

I didn't venture to ring the bell. I might be asked whether I'd had anything to do with a broken marble mantel over the living room fireplace. I hadn't done it, but the mantel had been broken and the biggest shard stuffed up the chimney. I didn't want any unpleasantness about that.

As I was turning to leave, the door opened and a teen-aged girl came out. She saw me looking at the house and asked, "Are you looking for someone?"

"No," I said. "I used to live here during the war for a while."

"Oh," she said, "what room did you have?"

"It was up there," I said, pointing to a window on the third floor. "Two of us stayed there."

"That's the maid's room," she said. "We're new here, so I don't know what it was before."

"A linen cupboard, probably," I said, and she giggled.

"What were you doing then?" she asked.

"I was flying from the airfield over there," I said, gesturing.

"An airfield?" she said. "I don't think I've heard about it."

"It's still there, but most of it is under the hay," I said.

"I must tell Mummy and Daddy," she said.

She skipped off towards a neighbor's and I walked to our old mess where we had eaten a steady diet of fish paste and Brussels sprouts. It was another large house, renovated now, sitting among lawns and trees and flowers. It smacked of smoked salmon and filet mignon. I didn't approach.

Just before I returned home from London, I paid a Sunday afternoon visit to the Chez Moi, a seedy basement club in Denman Street just a step away from the Regent Palace Hotel. It had been a favorite hangout during the war, mainly because it was so close to the Regent Palace and Piccadilly Circus. James was still behind the bar, but Old Sylvie was gone.

Old Sylvie used to play the piano softly and drink gin swiftly, until she slid off the stool and we carried her into a cubbyhole behind the bar and put her down gently on a cot kept there for that purpose. James said Old Sylvie had died in 1949, only a few days after falling off the stool for the last time.

The club was full of Canadian sailors off the aircraft carrier *Magnificent*, in England as part of the coronation celebrations. I sat down beside a young AB and asked him how the trip was going. He got up and walked away without saying a word, having been told by his mother (as mine had told me) not to talk to strange men in civilian clothes in big cities.

In 1979, a doctor whom I have outlived found that I had diabetes and put me on the wagon. Goodbye four fingers of rum, repeated until sleep under the newspaper by 8 p.m. Hello vista of long, sober, wide-awake evenings. "Now," said my wife, "is the time for you to put your typewriter where your mouth is."

The resulting book, *Terror in the Starboard Seat*, an account of my tour of operations with 418 Squadron, was published in the fall of 1980. W.H. Smith, the booksellers, thought it had to do with current commercial flying and put it on the transportation shelf. During a book promotion interview on a Vancouver television station, I found myself playing opposite a World Series game tied in the tenth inning. But Vancouver produced the shortest and best description of the book, which is about a gung-ho pilot and scared navigator (me). "Ah," said my good friend, Dave Stockand of the Vancouver *Sun*, "derring-do and derring-don't."

In 1981, Jean and I were in England on vacation, which included a search of Yorkshire for author-veterinarian James Herriot so that my wife could obtain his autograph on his latest book (and, surprisingly to me, so that she could present a signed copy of my book to him; she had discovered that he had been in the air force during the war). We even had lunch in the very same village pub, the Wheat Sheaf, where Herriot and his bride had spent their honeymoon. (My wife is a genuine Herriot nut.) The natives in the pub had seen the television series taken from the Herriot stories but didn't realize there was an actual Herriot. This led to a long and confusing conversation in front of the fireplace. We were informed that Herriot had been recently divorced; it turned out that the actors playing Mr. and Mrs. Herriot in the TV series had fallen for each other and divorced their spouses. The natives looked at us with deep suspicion when we said we had met Herriot the previous day in Thirsk, where he lived and practised. We decided not to send them over the brink by telling them that Herriot's real name is Wight.

We returned to the comparative sanity of London. John Murray Ltd. had bought the British rights to *Terror in the Starboard Seat* and was bringing it out soon. I phoned to ask whether we might call, and John Murray said they would be delighted.

John Murray has been in business since the 1760s and in the same building in Albemarle Street since 1812 or so. The firm was still run by a Murray, and another Murray was ready in the wings.

A very personable young man, Roger Hudson, escorted my wife and me up a long flight of stairs to his office, which had a ceiling at least 20 feet high. He showed us the new cover with new title for my book: *Mosquito Intruder*.

"The name of the plane sells books over here," he said. "Spitfire is No. 1, Mosquito is No. 2."

With our brief business transacted, Mr. Hudson (I don't think first names have ever been used in those premises) said, "Now, perhaps you'd like to meet some of your fellow authors." He showed us around two enormous rooms, the walls covered in portraits: Byron, Sir Walter Scott, Keats, Sir John Franklin. Even in jest, I didn't have the nerve to ask whether John Murray would like to have my portrait. Come to think of it, Mr. Hudson didn't ask whether I had a snap of myself.

I had had a long-standing pact with a friend in Vancouver to attend the next reunion of our squadron. When it was held in Toronto in the summer of 1982, I wasn't fussy about going. I'd never attended a reunion of any kind, but I'd agreed to go if Doug was going and sent in my down payment to the reunion committee. At the last moment Doug backed out—he wasn't shirking; he had sound, even plausible, reasons. Still fresh in face and young in step, I resigned myself to a weekend with fleshy, balding old coots who were probably all professional veterans. My wife volunteered to accompany me, and that helped. Indeed, spouses were more than welcome.

Our squadron had always been a close-knit, introspective unit during the war. That was partly because of its work; it was the only Canadian night-intruder squadron, making its shop talk almost exclusively internal. What brave and splendid deeds we would be recalling in that modern-drab hotel in far-west Toronto at the squadron's 40th anniversary.

Jean and I arrived at the drinks room late Friday afternoon. The first person I saw drew a blank. I didn't have the faintest idea who he was.

"Let's go home," I said to my wife. "I don't know anybody here."

"Remember your down payment," she said.

The man I didn't know and who, I noted resentfully, looked surprisingly young, presented a card: Al Day. What a relief. I didn't know him because he had completed his combat flying before I joined the squadron.

"Who did you fly with?" I asked Al, anxious to get right into the reminiscing.

He ignored the question. "What are you doing now?" he asked.

The second person I saw was, I thought, Mark Zimmer, a fellow navigator in the olden days. But it couldn't be. I said to Jean, "I didn't know the guys could be represented by their sons." I asked the fresh-faced kid, "Are you Mark Zimmer's son? You sure look like him."

Drat. It was Mark, hair still curly, no lines in his face.

"What do you think about what the government's doing on national energy?" he asked

Our discussion of the mess in Ottawa put a damper on any recounting of wartime exploits.

I wouldn't have thought it possible that I could recognize so many people after all that time. I had seen only a few since the war, like Russ Bannock, our commanding officer, and Ed McGill, with his wavy dark hair, both declining to age properly. But I hadn't seen those two hundred others. I'm not good at putting names to faces but I don't think I missed once that weekend, and I found that generally the case. Maybe in the war we were strung so high and so taut that everybody and everything were etched in memory forever.

I asked Don McLaren what he remembered especially.

"How many kids have you got and what are they doing?" he asked.

Jean, of course, was able to join in conversation like this. No wonder wives were encouraged to attend. All the talk was in the pregnant present.

Almost plaintively, I said to Don, "Why doesn't anybody talk about the war?"

"We all know how it came out," he said. "Now what is your next book going to be about?"

There were squadron members who never knew how the war came out, and we remembered them at the Saturday night banquet when the trumpeter played "Last Post." But we stepped back quickly from the graveside. The speaker of the evening talked not about the air force we had known but about the air element of our armed forces, or what's left of them. Perry Arnold, secretary of the reunion committee, without a backward glance rattled off plans for future reunions. Then it was on with the dance. I noticed Zimmer especially, whirling about the floor like Nureyev. I was about the only one who sat out some of the sets.

I made one last try. I said to Charlie Peake, "Do you remember a guy named Jensen?"

"Naw," Charlie said. "Say, do you ever come to Saskatchewan? After I got my poop and bangs equipment fixed, I got a nice little place on a lake near my farm. I can get off by myself with a case of beer and fish or read or do whatever I damn please."

If I go to another reunion—and I hope to, just to keep up with current affairs if nothing else—perhaps I'll also run into somebody who recalls the war.

One day in 1986 I read in the *Archivist*, published by the National Archives of Canada: "The records of all wartime veterans are kept indefinitely because of their heritage value."

My God, I thought, I'm going to be immortal. But if I was going to be making such an important contribution to national heritage, maybe I should take a look at my priceless file.

So I made an appointment to see it at the National Personnel Records Centre on Goldenrod Street in Tunney's Pasture, which is not a pasture at all but the biggest anthill of civil servants in Ottawa. I signed for my file and was sent to a desk in a cubicle that was like the ones people use in banks to gloat over the contents of their safety deposit boxes.

Allow me to cover the salient nuggets in this heritage treasure:

- W.R.S. Wilson, chief medical officer, No. 11 Recruiting Centre, RCAF, Toronto, wrote on my chart March 31, 1942: "Excellent material for air crew." Under that, Sqdn. Ldr. J.C. Whyte, medical officer, scrawled, but legibly enough: "Too tall for gunner." Here's to you, Dr. Whyte, though departed. The survival rate for air gunners in 1942 was near absolute zero.

- Between April 29 and June 16, 1942, I received 10 cc of vaccine, 1 cc at a time, and a medical opinion—unsought—that I have "little toes."

- I was given three days CB (confined to barracks) at No. 1 Air Observer School, Malton, Ontario, on February 1, 1943, for "conduct to the prejudice of good order and air force discipline in that he failed to rise at reveille (06:45 hours) and was found in bed at 07:55 hours by the barracks corporal." I was a wild one, all right.
- On arrival in England in April, 1943, I was issued 72 clothing coupons.
- The three books that I borrowed from the library at Bournemouth, England, were *The Making of Society*, *The Portugal of Salazar* and *So This Is Poland*. Authors not given.
- During a wireless course, I learned to operate the Aldis lamp at eight words a minute.
- My squadron CO put me down for a 6 in the category for "zeal and energy." Scale not given.
- A squadron form for "particulars of any bad experiences during tour" was blank. I suspect it was withheld from me on the supposition that I'd run off the page.
- My war service gratuity came to $708.24, paid in three monthly instalments.

Pretty exciting stuff, eh? But you'll just have to be patient. Nobody else is allowed to see my secret file till I'm dead or, rather, immortal but inaccessible.

The Wheatfield

There were eight of us in two cars, driving southwest from Saskatoon on a sunny late September morning: Neva's husband, Ted; her daughter, Margaret; her son, Tom; her granddaughter, Miranda; and two couples who were among Neva's closest friends, Betty and Al, and Jean and I.

By the time we reached Flaxcombe, after about two hours, a light rain was falling. Flaxcombe sits in a wide, north-south valley. We drove down through the village and halfway up the rise on the other side. Ted and Al stopped their cars beside a wheatfield that Neva had chosen as her burial ground. She had made the selection years before, long before she knew about the cancer of the heart that killed her. She had had time to study the land during the long drives between Calgary, where she lived, and Biggar, Saskatchewan, her unloved hometown which she still visited regularly until her parents died. The land around Flaxcombe was slightly rolling and broken, as it was around Biggar.

We got out of the cars and put on our raincoats or jackets. Ted took the urn with Neva's ashes out of the trunk of his car, and the eight of us walked through the shallow ditch beside the road and into the unfenced field. It had been cut not long before and there were muddy spots among the three-inch yellow stubble. I suddenly remembered running with my young cousins through fresh stubble in a wheatfield (much smaller, of course) on my uncle's farm in New Brunswick. We dared each other to do it; you had to run as fast as you could because the stubble was as stiff as a wire brush, and if you slowed down it felt as if you were walking on one.

We were some distance from the road when Ted said, "I guess this will be the place." Alders and willows surrounded the field on three sides. There was no farmhouse, no piece of machinery, no other human in the wide landscape; just the telephone poles marching up over the rise towards Alsask and the Alberta border.

We huddled together, touching shoulders and arms, in the wet field, and Ted said, his voice stumbling, "Neva, may you rest in peace forever," and then he shook some white ashes out of the brown urn into each one's cupped hands. We spread apart and, more or less at the same time, threw them into the soft rain. Ted scattered the rest himself, walking this way and that among the stubble. Tears mixed with rain on our faces. But the tears were the kind that mothers shed at a daughter's wedding: a leave-taking that is a celebration. "It was wonderful," Neva's son said simply as we straggled back to the cars, the mud growing on our shoes. The ones who had cameras wiped the rain off the lenses and took snaps of the empty wheatfield. Ted put the urn back in the trunk.

We got the cars turned around easily in the deserted road, and by the time we were all seated in the restaurant in Kindersley—there was a table large enough for all of us—we were smiling and chatting as if Neva were there, and pleased that we had carried out her funereal wish, to the letter.

On the way back to Saskatoon, Ted, Jean and I—the others went directly back in Al's car—cut north from Rosetown to Biggar. "I just want you to see where Neva was brought up," Ted said.

Biggar is a dispirited town since it ceased to be a divisional point on the CNR. Ted pointed out the mean, cramped house where Neva had lived with her parents and seven brothers and sisters. We went to the rundown hotel and into the beer parlor where the TV set was showing Olympic weightlifting for a small crowd of patrons in baseball caps.

"We used to stay here when we visited," Ted said. "I wasn't sorry when we didn't have to come any more." He looked around, and his look seemed to take in the hotel, the railroad and the town.

"Neva surmounted all this," he said. "She got away, to Saskatoon, and Vancouver, and London, and Brazil, and Edmonton and Calgary, and after her parents died she never wanted to come back."

The next day, Ted, Margaret, Jean and I drove to Calgary. We stopped again beside the road on the rise out of Flaxcombe and took some more pictures of Neva's wheatfield, because it was sunny.

The Street Where I Stood

Jean and I decided we needed a winter break from Ottawa.

So we flew to Halifax and into the mixed bag of misery which passes for its February weather: some fog; some rain, light and heavy; one freezing gale; a snatch or two of sun; one cold snap; some snow; all within 48 hours.

But we had a reason: sentiment. We had been married in Halifax 40 years earlier (February 18, 1950, to be precise) in a Roman Catholic rectory—"out behind the garbage cans," my Protestant mother said. Jean and I have never regretted the ceremony or the marriage. We haven't even had a trial separation.

We had a courtship of more than three years, conducted mainly on Hollis Street in Halifax. Hastily, I add that it had no connection with one of the street's chief trades: prostitution. I worked nights (about 4 p.m. to 3 a.m.—there were no set hours) in the shabby but happy Canadian Press office opposite Province House (the legislative building). I lived for a year or so in one room in a walkup apartment in a rundown tenement (miraculously, still standing) near the south end of Hollis Street where it debouches into the railway station. The only people who picked me up were the police. I had a canvas suitcase to send my laundry home to my mother in Quebec and the clean wash came back in the same case, sometimes with gingersnaps. This postal operation saved money; my landlady, Mrs. Lutz, was writing the longest unpublished novel in the history of literature and had no time to accept laundry assignments. I used the office as my mailing address, and often late at night I'd be lugging my laundry case home. The police were forever stopping me and asking me what was in the bag. I'd tell them but, every time, they had to look. Under their flashlights (sometimes as many as four) I'd undo the straps and expose the shining results of my mother's scrubbing. I'll give the cops this: they never poked around in the clean clothes, they never stole my gingersnaps and they never ran me in as a fetishist.

Near the far north end of Hollis Street was the rear wall of Wood Brothers' big department store where Jean was secretary to the boss. In the thick stone wall was the employees' entrance. Jean worked until 5:30 p.m. (noon on Saturday). I took my food break at Canadian Press at about 5:30, though CP preferred the staff to eat sandwiches at the desk (there was only one), and dashed down to Woods' employees' entrance to await Jean's exit.

Usually, I walked her home, but in bad weather, and provided I was flush with savings from my pay of 30 dollars a week, we took the Barrington-Spring Garden streetcar. She lived with her parents and sisters at 180 Robie Street, a house since taken over by Dalhousie University and renumbered 1312 (the street must have grown longer at one or both ends). Her mother often took pity on me (I cut a fairly pitiful figure) and whipped some food into me before I rushed back to the office. Otherwise, it was the all-night Chinese Atomic Cafe.

On Saturdays in the summer, we often went to Wanderers' Grounds and sat in the cool of the maple trees overhanging the wooden stands and watched the local heroes play against the Liverpool Larrupers or some other team in what was a good semi-pro baseball league. Sometimes it was a movie. Once in a long while I saved enough for a case of beer. If Jean could get her father's car or if a friend-with-car came along, several of us would pile in and drive to Hubbard's or Queensland where we'd sit on the beach with a beer and crack fresh-cooked lobsters (25 cents each—15 cents for small ones). A real razzmatazz evening was the dinner-dance at the Nova Scotian Hotel but for that I had to find money in the street or wait for at least two CP raises, which ranged from two to three dollars a week.

Saturday night was my only night off so that most of my courting was the evening patrol on a small section of pavement of Hollis Street behind Woods' department store waiting for Jean and walking my red-haired true-love home. Sometimes, when we had a spat, she wouldn't come out at quitting time but leave me pacing and fuming outside (and denied her mother's cooking). During one extended quarrel, I didn't go down to the store at all, then found myself peering round corners into Barrington Street hoping to catch a secret glimpse of her in the tram or walking home, laughing, with her friends.

We often go back to Nova Scotia, but in summer or fall, especially fall when we can walk alone the long white beaches of Melmerby, Port Hood, Ingonish, Spry Harbor, Bayswater and my favorite spot on earth, Clam Harbor, where the surf forever roars softly as if trapped in a barrel.

We always visit Mary MacKenzie Smith, Jean's oldest friend (they have been as thick as thieves since they were eight-year-olds in New Glasgow). Mary is a recent widow. Her husband, Art, knew everybody in Nova Scotia—I don't mean everybody who was somebody, I mean everybody—and his ashes are buried in downtown Halifax, where he worked and where he wanted to stay, right up against the south wall of St. David's Presbyterian Church. The minister of St. David's, Rev. John Pace, said the site was doubly fitting: not only was Art downtown, but he had parked illegally for years in the church lot near his law office.

We always see Mary first, and in February, 1990, as in other seasons and other years, she greeted us at home with love, lobster and a perfectly chilled white wine. Mary and Jean talked feverishly, though they had been talking not fifteen minutes before on the cab's cellular phone while we were on our way in from the airport.

The next morning, I sought out my old stamping ground (it was that, literally, in cold weather) on the sidewalk on Hollis Street. It was there all right, but a bank has replaced Wood Bros. The rear wall was entirely blank: no door of any kind, not even for tradesmen. Jean took a snap anyway of me standing in the grooves I'd worn in Hollis Street so long ago.

As we drove to the airport to go home, Jean said to me, "Well, we spent more time in our hotel room this time than we did on our honeymoon, but unfortunately not for the same reason."

February weather in Halifax tends to keep one indoors.